So you really want to learn

Maths
Prep

BOOK 2
Answer Book

ISEB

Independent Schools
Examinations Board

GALORE PARK

Published by ISEB Publications, an imprint of
Galore Park Publishing Ltd,
PO Box 96, Cranbrook, Kent TN17 4WS
www.galorepark.co.uk

Text copyright © Galore Park
Illustrations copyright © Galore Park 2004
Technical drawings by Graham Edwards

This publication includes images from CorelDRAW ® 9 which are
protected by the copyright laws of the U.S., Canada and elsewhere.
Used under licence.

Typography and layout by Typetechnique, London W1
Cover design by GKA Design, London WC2H
Printed by The Bath Press

ISBN 1 902984 32 3

First published 2004

Maths Prep Book 1 Pupil's Book	ISBN 1 902984 18 8
Maths Prep Book 1 Answer Book	ISBN 1 902984 19 6
Maths Prep Book 1 Worksheets CD	ISBN 1 902984 49 8
Maths Prep Book 2 Pupil's Book	ISBN 1 902984 31 5
Maths Prep Book 2 Answer Book	ISBN 1 902984 32 3
Maths Prep Book 2 Worksheets CD	ISBN 1 902984 54 4

Available in the series:
English Prep
Latin Prep
French Prep
Maths Prep
Science Prep

Preface

The publishers would like once again to thank David Hanson of the ISEB for his invaluable help during the production of this book. Serena and all of us at Galore Park are most grateful.

Contents

Chapter 1: Working with numbers

This chapter should be done without a calculator, however pupils who have a scientific calculator could be allowed to CHECK their answers with their calculator.

Exercise 1.1: A challenge

A mental warm up to start the new academic year.

1.
(a) 5 + 2 = 7
(b) 6 + 3 = 9
(c) 8 + 1 = 9
(d) 4 + 3 = 7
(e) 5 + 4 = 9

(f) 15 + 82 = 97
(g) 36 + 43 = 79
(h) 28 + 71 = 99
(i) 24 + 53 = 77
(j) 65 + 24 = 89

2.
(a) 5 + 9 = 14
(b) 8 + 3 = 11
(c) 7 + 6 = 13
(d) 9 + 4 = 13
(e) 6 + 5 = 11

(f) 25 + 39 = 64
(g) 18 + 73 = 91
(h) 57 + 36 = 93
(i) 29 + 64 = 93
(j) 46 + 35 = 81

3.
(a) 9 − 5 = 4
(b) 5 − 3 = 2
(c) 6 − 1 = 5
(d) 7 − 4 = 3
(e) 8 − 6 = 2

(f) 39 − 15 = 24
(g) 65 − 33 = 32
(h) 86 − 21 = 65
(i) 47 − 14 = 33
(j) 58 − 46 = 12

4.
(a) 12 − 4 = 8
(b) 16 − 7 = 9
(c) 11 − 2 = 9
(d) 13 − 8 = 5
(e) 15 − 7 = 8

(f) 42 − 34 = 8
(g) 56 − 27 = 29
(h) 91 − 22 = 69
(i) 33 − 28 = 5
(j) 65 − 17 = 48

5.
(a) 35 + 15 = 50
(b) 45 + 14 = 59
(c) 66 + 23 = 89
(d) 47 + 13 = 60
(e) 23 + 37 = 60

(f) 65 − 36 = 29
(g) 27 − 18 = 9
(h) 63 − 24 = 39
(i) 68 − 49 = 19
(j) 44 − 35 = 9

6.
(a) 19 + 5 = 24
(b) 35 + 29 = 64
(c) 67 + 19 = 86
(d) 49 + 37 = 86
(e) 43 + 59 = 102

(f) 56 − 29 = 27
(g) 32 − 19 = 13
(h) 81 − 59 = 22
(i) 64 − 49 = 15
(j) 77 − 69 = 8

7.
(a) 121 + 48 = 169
(b) 325 + 124 = 449
(c) 313 + 116 = 429
(d) 135 + 124 = 259
(e) 342 + 327 = 669
(f) 165 − 23 = 142
(g) 332 − 121 = 211
(h) 467 − 235 = 232
(i) 635 − 124 = 511
(j) 757 − 131 = 626

8.
(a) 147 + 45 = 192
(b) 356 + 124 = 480
(c) 384 + 123 = 507
(d) 175 + 352 = 527
(e) 616 + 347 = 963
(f) 452 − 25 = 427
(g) 657 − 163 = 494
(h) 318 − 235 = 83
(i) 452 − 361 = 91
(j) 456 − 264 = 192

9.
(a) 156 + 76 = 232
(b) 485 + 173 = 658
(c) 293 + 239 = 532
(d) 376 + 186 = 562
(e) 145 + 567 = 712
(f) 164 − 85 = 79
(g) 457 − 268 = 189
(h) 461 − 178 = 283
(i) 637 − 358 = 279
(j) 378 − 289 = 89

10.
(a) 243 + 167 = 410
(b) 345 + 567 = 912
(c) 567 + 123 = 690
(d) 319 + 399 = 718
(e) 678 + 398 = 1076
(f) 402 − 123 = 279
(g) 607 − 288 = 319
(h) 308 − 159 = 149
(i) 402 − 361 = 41
(j) 706 − 358 = 348

Exercise 1.2

1.	399	**6.**	6190	**11.**	4092
2.	705	**7.**	4436	**12.**	559
3.	1015	**8.**	1241	**13.**	1825
4.	424	**9.**	4715	**14.**	7219
5.	383	**10.**	10026	**15.**	1434

Exercise 1.3

It is surprising how many children get to aged 11 or 12 and still have trouble with subtraction. Check their setting out and exchanged numbers carefully.

1.	361	**6.**	2768	**11.**	148
2.	314	**7.**	4863	**12.**	114
3.	515	**8.**	8634	**13.**	1604
4.	263	**9.**	278	**14.**	333
5.	346	**10.**	3017	**15.**	357

Exercise 1.4: Multiplication

1.

×	10	2	3	5	9	4	6	11	8	12	7
5	50	10	15	25	45	20	30	55	40	60	35
10	100	20	30	50	90	40	60	110	80	120	70
7	70	14	21	35	63	28	42	77	56	84	49
9	90	18	27	45	81	36	54	99	72	108	63
2	20	4	6	10	18	8	12	22	16	24	14
8	80	16	24	40	72	32	48	88	64	96	56
4	40	8	12	20	36	16	24	44	32	48	28
11	110	22	33	55	99	44	66	121	88	132	77
12	120	24	36	60	108	48	72	132	96	144	84
3	30	6	9	15	27	12	18	33	24	36	21
6	60	12	18	30	54	24	36	66	48	72	42

2. 28
3. 152
4. 250
5. 57
6. 350

7. 285
8. 420
9. 651
10. 297
11. 1791

Exercise 1.5: Division

1. (a) $55 \div 5 = 11$
(b) $40 \div 5 = 8$
(c) $18 \div 3 = 6$
(d) $56 \div 8 = 7$
(e) $63 \div 7 = 9$
(f) $28 \div 4 = 7$
(g) $54 \div 9 = 6$
(h) $35 \div 5 = 7$
(i) $49 \div 7 = 7$
(j) $32 \div 8 = 4$

2. (a) $63 \div 6 = 10 \text{ r}3$
(b) $13 \div 2 = 6 \text{ r}1$
(c) $25 \div 7 = 3 \text{ r}4$
(d) $43 \div 8 = 5 \text{ r}3$
(e) $36 \div 5 = 7 \text{ r}1$
(f) $29 \div 3 = 9 \text{ r}2$
(g) $35 \div 4 = 8 \text{ r}3$
(h) $49 \div 9 = 5 \text{ r}4$
(i) $26 \div 6 = 4 \text{ r}2$
(j) $59 \div 7 = 8 \text{ r}3$

3. (a) $21 \div 3 = 7$
(b) $45 \div 7 = 6 \text{ r}3$
(c) $24 \div 6 = 4$
(d) $49 \div 8 = 6 \text{ r}1$
(e) $31 \div 4 = 7 \text{ r}3$
(f) $39 \div 9 = 4 \text{ r}3$
(g) $60 \div 5 = 12$
(h) $19 \div 2 = 9 \text{ r}1$
(i) $37 \div 7 = 5 \text{ r}2$
(j) $56 \div 8 = 7$

Exercise 1.6: Estimation

1.	60	6.	30
2.	600	7.	100
3.	1000	8.	5000
4.	90	9.	100
5.	5000	10.	1000

Slightly different answers are acceptable if they have rounded 1432 to say 1400, not 1000.

11.	6000 (6976)	16.	70 000 (91 750)
12.	40 000 (35 550)	17.	2 000 000 (2 095 800)
13.	24 000 (26 789)	18.	60 000 (62 964)
14.	100 000 (108 900)	19.	45 000 (41 424)
15.	600 000 (899 296)	20.	3 000 000 (2 985 147)

21.	20 (16.63)	26.	4 (3.60)
22.	35 (42.88)	27.	8 (8.42)
23.	20 (17.77)	28.	40 (36.48)
24.	9 (8.23)	29.	20 (22.58)
25.	20 (19.70)	30.	20 (21.05)

31. (Exact numbers shown in brackets.)

Exercise 1.7: Multiplication

1.	72	6.	1225
2.	78	7.	1672
3.	148	8.	2934
4.	215	9.	3336
5.	948	10.	3752

11.	480	16.	9180
12.	12 800	17.	196 000
13.	2700	18.	28 440
14.	11 700	19.	449 400
15.	6300	20.	411 300

Exercise 1.8: Long multiplication

These should have been done without a calculator and showing all the working.

1.	840	6.	2125	11.	864 packets
2.	2412	7.	6344	12.	13 040 pages
3.	1215	8.	23 400	13.	£20 000
4.	3402	9.	14 283	14.	14 400 seconds
5.	2304	10.	55 848	15.	204 pounds

Exercise 1.9: Short division

1.	13	6.	119
2.	16	7.	107
3.	26 r1	8.	113 r4
4.	63	9.	103 r2
5.	53 r4	10.	141

11. 4 (210 children went.)
12. 4 (144 are on plates - 24 on each plate.)
13. 1 table of 40, 5 tables of 42.
14. 23 in each of the top 2 classes.

Exercise 1.10: Long division

These calculations should be done by long division.

1. 38
2. 29
3. 45
4. 21
5. 23

6. 36 r6
7. 19
8. 32 r3
9. 36
10. 18 r28

11. 17 chocolates each
12. £34
13. 13 minutes
14. 75p
15. 20 each and 20 left over

Exercise 1.11: Mixed questions

1. 12p
2. 25p
3. 224 ounces
4. 574 points
5. 140 children
6. 15 children
7. 64 m
8. 56 balls

9. £132
10. 12 750 minutes, 212 and a half hours
11. 125 g, 4500 g
12. 25 weeks
13. 1545 g
14. (a) £318   (b) 15
15. £3224

Exercise 1.12: Mixed operations

1. 23
2. 0
3. 32
4. 8
5. 11

6. 4
7. 3
8. 27
9. 16
10. 81

11. $(4 + 7) \times 6 = 66$
12. $(9 - 5) \div 2 = 2$
13. $34 \div 2 - 5 = 12$
14. $12^2 \div 2 = 72$

Exercise 1.13: Extension exercise – Babylonian numbers

This is just a taster of the interesting topic of the cuneiform numbers, and other number bases. There is plenty of opportunity here for further research and some cross curricular work with History, Geography and Classics.

1. (a) 4
   (b) 14

   (c) 59
   (d) 63

   (e) 126
   (f) 83

2. (a) 6

   (c) 56

   (e) 75

   (g) 127

   (b) 26

   (d) 64

   (f) 92
   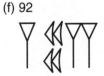

   (h) 142

3.   (a) 184   (c) 179   (e) 359
        (b) 344   (d) 1292   (f) 3296

4.   (a) 306

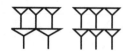

(b) 2472

(c) 2364

(d) 1317

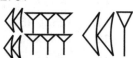

(e) 3216

(f) 2781

(g) 1204

(h) 3599

5.   (a) 3812   (c) 374 570
        (b) 8696   (d) 10 409

6.   (a) 3666

(b) 7297

(c) 4876

(d) 5999

7.   Time, 60 seconds in a minute, 60 minutes in an hour.

Exercise 1.14: Summary exercise

1. 485
2. 613
3. 632
4. 244
5. 195

6. 9
7. 8 r5
8. 8000
9. 150
10. 102

Check the pupils have given an estimate to the following questions:

11. 15 000
12. 1 000 000

13. 200
14. 7 or 8 ($7\frac{1}{2}$)

Make sure the answers have been carefully calculated in frames:

15. 5979
16. 6328
17. 1554

18. 17 523
19. 114 r3
20. 34 r23

21. £12 or £13 - suggest £13 otherwise the school is £336 out of pocket!
22. 563 potatoes
23. 35 Euros
24. 936 words
25. £9360
26. 228
27. 617

End of chapter 1 activity: Dice games

You can devise your own variations to these games. Using dice with 8 or more faces makes an interesting change.

Chapter 2: Back to Babylon

Exercise 2.1

1. (a) 216-Yes   (b) 480-Yes   (c) 425-No   (d) 614-No   (e) 12 324-Yes

2. (a) 216-Yes   (b) 891-Yes   (c) 617-No   (d) 6138-Yes   (e) 19 368-Yes

3. (a) 7-Yes   (b) 27-No   (c) 77-Yes   (d) 717-No   (e) 91-Yes

4. (a) 88-Yes   (b) 121-Yes   (c) 292-No   (d) 374-Yes   (e) 2574-Yes

5.
   - (a) 3   1, 3
   - (b) 37   1, 37
   - (c) 71   1, 71
   - (d) 83   1, 83
   - (e) 101   1, 101

6.
   - (a) 1   1
   - (b) 25   1, 5, 25
   - (c) 64   1, 2, 4, 8, 16, 32, 64
   - (d) 9   1, 3, 9
   - (e) 144   1, 2, 3, 4, 6, 8, 12, 18, 24, 36, 48, 72, 144

7.
   - (a) 10   1, 2, 5, 10
   - (b) 16   1, 2, 4, 8, 16
   - (c) 24   1, 2, 3, 4, 6, 8, 12, 24
   - (d) 60   1, 2, 3, 4, 5, 6, 10, 12, 15, 20, 30, 60
   - (e) 100   1, 2, 4, 5, 10, 20, 25, 50, 100

8. It has a lot of factors.

Exercise 2.2

1. 2   3   5   7   11   13   17   19   23   29
   31   37   41   43   47

2. (a) 87-No   (b) 91-No   (c) 107-Yes   (d) 207-No   (e) 231-No

3.
   - (a) $16 = 2 \times 2 \times 2 \times 2$
   - (b) $40 = 2 \times 2 \times 2 \times 5$
   - (c) $120 = 2 \times 2 \times 2 \times 3 \times 5$
   - (d) $28 = 2 \times 2 \times 7$
   - (e) $100 = 2 \times 2 \times 5 \times 5$

4.
   - (a) $16 = 2^4$
   - (b) $40 = 2^3 \times 5$
   - (c) $120 = 2^3 \times 3 \times 5$
   - (d) $28 = 2^2 \times 7$
   - (e) $100 = 2^2 \times 5^2$

5.
   - (a) 18
   - (b) 36
   - (c) 360
   - (d) 900
   - (e) 2200

6. (a) $2^2 \times 3^2 \times 7$ (d) $3^3 \times 5^2 \times 17$
   (b) $3 \times 5 \times 7 \times 11$ (e) $5 \times 11 \times 113$
   (c) $2 \times 3 \times 7 \times 19$

7. (a) 3   (b) 8   (c) 20

8. (a) 40   (b) 80   (c) 100

Exercise 2.3

1. (a) 24   (c) 36   (e) 80
   (b) 66   (d) 56   (f) 126

2. (a) 180   (b) 720   (c) 360   (d) 2016   (e) 3200   (f) 4410

3. (a) 84   (d) 96
   (b) 24   (e) 90
   (c) 99

   (f) Primes 2   3   5   7   11   13   17   19   23   29
                 31   37   41   43   47   53   59   61   67
                 71   73   79   83   89   93   97

   (g) Squares 1, 4, 9, 16, 25, 36, 49, 64, 81, 100
   (h) 90
   (i) 19
   (j) 10

Exercise 2.4

1. (a) $4^2 = 16$ (b) $2^2 = 4$ (c) $6^2 = 36$

2. (a) 49   (b) 81   (c) 121
3. 1, 4, 9, 16, 25, 36, 49, 64, 81, 100
4. (a) 48, 63, 80
   (b) One less than a square number.
5. (a) 51, 66, 83
   (b) 2 more than a square number.
6. [0,] 1, 4, 9, 16, 25, 36, 49, 64, 81, 100 – it actually says starts with zero but zero should <u>not</u> be written down. They are square numbers.
7. 7
8. (a) 4   (b) 2   (c) 6
9. Evaluate (a long word meaning 'find the value of')
   (a) 10   (b) 9   (c) 1   (d) 5   (e) 8   (f) 12
10. $9 + 16 = 25$
     $36 + 64 = 100$

11. The largest angle is 90°.

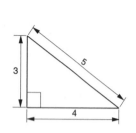

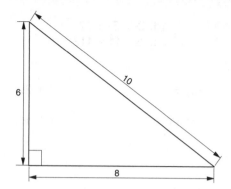

Exercise 2.5

1. (a) 8 (b) 27 (c) 64

2.

n	n^3
1	1
2	8
3	27
4	64
5	125
6	216
7	343
8	512
9	729
10	1000
11	1331
12	1728

3. (a) 2 (b) 5 (c) 10
4. (a) 4 (b) 9 (c) 6 (d) 7 (e) 8
5. 1 and 64
6. No!

Exercise 2.6: Triangle numbers

1. 1, 3, 6, 10, 15, 21, 28, 36, 45, 55

2. The sums of the pairs are square numbers.

3. For example:

4. Multiply each triangle number by 9 and add 1
    $9 \times T_1 + 1 = 9 \times 1 + 1 = 10 = T_4$
    $9 \times T_2 + 1 = 28 = T_7$
    $9 \times T_3 + 1 = 55 = T_{10}$
    $9 \times T_4 + 1 = 91 = T_{13}$
    $9 \times T_5 + 1 = 136 = T_{16}$ etc

5. 66, 78, 91, 105, 120

    1, 3, 6, 0, 5, 1, 8, 6, 5, 5, 6, 8, 1, 5, 0
    No 2, 4, 7, 9
    Pairs make 5, 4, 9, 6, 14, 11, 10, only. (Note: if this is continued then we get a pair sum of 1
    (171 + 190) and a pair sum of (190 + 210)

6. 1, 3, 6, 1, 6, 3, 1, 9, 9, 1, 3, 6, 1, 6, 3
    Apart from 9 only 1, 3 and 6, triangle numbers themselves!

7. Multiply each triangle number by 8 and add 1
    $8 \times T_1 + 1 = 8 \times 1 + 1 = 9$
    $8 \times T_2 + 1 = 25$
    $8 \times T_3 + 1 = 49$
    $8 \times T_4 + 1 = 81$
    $8 \times T_5 + 1 = 121$ etc

    The results are all squares.

8. One side is always 1 unit longer than the other.
9. You get triangle numbers.
10. (a) $10 \times 11 \div 2 = 55$ (b) $20 \times 21 \div 2 = 210$ (c) $100 \times 101 \div 2 = 5050$

Exercise 2.7

1. Multiples of numbers ending in 2:
$2 \times 6 = 12$	$2 \times 11 = 22$	$3 \times 4 = 12$	$4 \times 3 = 12$
$4 \times 8 = 32$	$6 \times 2 = 12$	$6 \times 7 = 42$	$6 \times 12 = 72$
$7 \times 6 = 42$	$8 \times 4 = 32$	$8 \times 9 = 72$	$9 \times 8 = 72$
$11 \times 2 = 22$	$11 \times 12 = 132$	$12 \times 6 = 72$	$12 \times 11 = 132$

2. Multiples of numbers ending in 3:
$3 \times 11 = 33$	$7 \times 9 = 63$	$9 \times 7 = 63$	$11 \times 3 = 33$

3. (a) Multiples of numbers ending in 4:
$2 \times 2 = 4$	$2 \times 7 = 14$	$2 \times 12 = 24$	$3 \times 8 = 24$
$4 \times 6 = 24$	$4 \times 11 = 44$	$6 \times 9 = 54$	$7 \times 2 = 14$
$7 \times 12 = 84$	$8 \times 3 = 24$	$8 \times 8 = 64$	$9 \times 6 = 54$
$11 \times 4 = 44$	$12 \times 2 = 24$	$12 \times 7 = 84$	$12 \times 12 = 144$

(b) Multiples of numbers ending in 5:

$3 \times 5 = 15$	$5 \times 3 = 15$	$5 \times 5 = 25$	$5 \times 7 = 35$
$5 \times 9 = 45$	$5 \times 11 = 55$	$7 \times 5 = 35$	$11 \times 5 = 55$

(c) Multiples of numbers ending in 6:

$2 \times 3 = 6$	$2 \times 8 = 16$	$3 \times 2 = 6$	$3 \times 12 = 36$
$4 \times 4 = 16$	$4 \times 9 = 36$	$6 \times 6 = 36$	$6 \times 11 = 66$
$7 \times 8 = 56$	$8 \times 2 = 16$	$8 \times 7 = 56$	$8 \times 12 = 96$
$9 \times 4 = 36$	$11 \times 6 = 66$	$12 \times 3 = 36$	$12 \times 8 = 96$

(d) Multiples of numbers ending in 7:

$3 \times 9 = 27$	$7 \times 11 = 77$	$9 \times 3 = 27$	$11 \times 7 = 77$

(e) Multiples of numbers ending in 8:

$2 \times 4 = 8$	$2 \times 9 = 18$	$3 \times 6 = 18$	$4 \times 2 = 8$
$4 \times 7 = 28$	$4 \times 12 = 48$	$6 \times 3 = 18$	$6 \times 8 = 48$
$7 \times 4 = 28$	$8 \times 6 = 48$	$8 \times 11 = 88$	$9 \times 2 = 18$
$9 \times 12 = 108$	$11 \times 8 = 88$	$12 \times 4 = 48$	$12 \times 9 = 108$

(f) Multiples of numbers ending in 9:

$3 \times 3 = 9$	$7 \times 7 = 49$	$9 \times 11 = 99$	$11 \times 9 = 99$

(g) Multiples of numbers ending in 0:

$2 \times 5 = 10$	$2 \times 10 = 20$	$3 \times 10 = 30$	$4 \times 5 = 20$
$4 \times 10 = 40$	$5 \times 2 = 10$	$5 \times 4 = 20$	$5 \times 6 = 30$
$5 \times 8 = 40$	$5 \times 10 = 50$	$5 \times 12 = 60$	$6 \times 5 = 30$
$6 \times 10 = 60$	$7 \times 10 = 70$	$8 \times 5 = 40$	$8 \times 10 = 80$
$9 \times 10 = 90$	$10 \times 2 = 20$	$10 \times 3 = 30$	$10 \times 4 = 40$
$10 \times 5 = 50$	$10 \times 6 = 60$	$10 \times 7 = 70$	$10 \times 8 = 80$
$10 \times 9 = 90$	$10 \times 10 = 100$	$10 \times 11 = 110$	$10 \times 12 = 120$
$11 \times 10 = 110$	$12 \times 5 = 60$	$12 \times 10 = 120$	

(h) Multiples of numbers ending in 1:

$3 \times 7 = 21$	$7 \times 3 = 21$	$9 \times 9 = 81$	$11 \times 11 = 121$

4. (a) 1 times (b) 2 times (c) Prime numbers

5. (a) 5 (b) 2 (c) 5 (d) 2 (e) 4 (f) 2

6.
(a) $31 \times 99 =$ (i) 3069 (ii) 2699 too small (iii) 2708 last digit
(b) $29 \times 42 =$ (i) 818 too small (ii) 1029 last digit (iii) 1218
(c) $31 \times 58 =$ (i) 1058 too small (ii) 1798 (iii) 1218 too small
(d) $78 \times 52 =$ (i) 4056 (ii) 456 too small (iii) 35 016 too big
(e) $72 \times 51 =$ (i) 3616 last digit (ii) 3492 too small (iii) 3672
(f) $99 \times 39 =$ (i) 2718 last digit (ii) 3861 (iii) 4081 too big

7. Pupils should have checked their answers to Q6 with their calculators.

8.
(a) $37 \times 25 = 925$ (d) $32 \times 49 = 1568$
(b) $29 \times 78 = 2262$ (e) $29 \times 58 = 1682$
(c) $45 \times 87 = 3915$ (f) $81 \times 61 = 4941$

Exercise 2.8

1. 6
2. 13
3. 4
4. £3
5. 36
6. 24
7. £43.20
8. 23 days
9. £2
10. 105 (105 is 35 rows of 5, or 21 rows of 5 or 15 rows of 7) or 106 (106 is 53 rows of 2)

Exercise 2.9: Pythagoras' perfect numbers

1.
$$6 = 1 + 2 + 3$$
$$28 = 1 + 2 + 4 + 7 + 14$$
$$496 = 1 + 2 + 4 + 8 + 16 + 31 + 62 + 124 + 248$$
$$8128 = 1 + 2 + 4 + 8 + 16 + 32 + 64 + 127 + 254 + 508 + 1016 + 2032 + 4064$$

2. 28 is a perfect number. In fact if you take 4 weeks of 7 days you get 28.
   4 is square and 7 is a prime number.

3. (a) There are 10 laws of Moses – triangle
   (b) 7 is lucky – prime
   (c) You come of age at 21- triangle
   (d) The French refer to a fortnight as 'quinze jours' (15 days) – triangle
   (e) The Romans had 10 months of 36 days (at one point!) lots of factors. 36 is both a square and triangle.

   Check the pupils' answers, but examples of other special numbers could include:

   1 very special – in religious terms the concept of one god is symbolic.

   2 the only even prime, one more than one.

   3 both a square and a triangle number and a number that recurs frequently in folklore and fable. Interestingly, it is the sum of 1 and 2, so therefore the origin of the trinity of god and man.

   4 square, and if you ignore 1, the first perfect square. We say there are four weeks in a month, even though there are four and a bit. Four gospels, four seasons, four elements etc.

   5 prime, wards off evil spirits – see Pythagoras below. Also five fingers on one hand, five senses, David took five stones to slay Goliath, etc.

   6 is perfect and a triangle. Strangely enough, we do not benefit much from this, although four of the months have 30 days which is 5 times 6. Remember that, according to Genesis, God made the world in 6 days (the 7th was for rest), so it was a perfect time frame. The star of David has six points to it, not five.

   7 prime and lucky, possibly because of the 7th day being for rest. Snow White and the 7 dwarfs, 7 deadly sins, etc.

8 is a cube. Eight days was a well used term before the seven day week became standard. Interestingly, the symbol for eight is regarded as magic because of its eternal spiral. You can make the whole number without removing your pen from the paper, and therefore go on writing eight for eternity. Of course, if you turn eight sideways then you get the sign for infinity…

9 is a square.

10 is a triangle, and happens to be the number of fingers and toes that we have. An interesting feature of ten is that it is the sum of 1, 3 and 6, the previous triangle numbers, and it also makes a spiral of squares. A magical number indeed. Note also the ten commandments.

11 prime, but rarely used symbolically.

12 a dozen, the product of three and four and thus all the magic of those two numbers. Note also the 12 disciples.

Forty is another biblical number that crops up with frequency. Forty days is a traditional number of discipline, devotion, and preparation in the Bible e.g. Moses stayed on the Mountain for forty days; Nineveh was given forty days to repent (Jonah 3:4); Jesus spent forty days in the wilderness praying and fasting and therefore there are forty days in lent etc.

Funnily enough, forty is neither prime, triangular, nor perfect, but Pythagoras is rumoured to have died on a forty day fast.

It is interesting to consider the Pythagorean definition of numbers, especially as he was obviously not a Christian, as many of the numbers have similar meanings.

Exercise 2.10: Extension questions

1. Complete these multiplication tables:

$1 \times 25 = 25$	$1 \times 125 = 125$	$1 \times 225 = 225$
$2 \times 25 = 50$	$2 \times 125 = 250$	$2 \times 225 = 450$
$3 \times 25 = 75$	$3 \times 125 = 375$	$3 \times 225 = 675$
$4 \times 25 = 100$	$4 \times 125 = 500$	$4 \times 225 = 900$
$5 \times 25 = 125$	$5 \times 125 = 625$	$5 \times 225 = 1125$
$6 \times 25 = 150$	$6 \times 125 = 750$	$6 \times 225 = 1350$
$7 \times 25 = 175$	$7 \times 125 = 875$	$7 \times 225 = 1575$
$8 \times 25 = 200$	$8 \times 125 = 1000$	$8 \times 225 = 1800$
$9 \times 25 = 225$	$9 \times 125 = 1125$	$9 \times 225 = 2025$
$10 \times 25 = 250$	$10 \times 125 = 1250$	$10 \times 225 = 2250$

2. $24 \times 19 = 24 \times (20 - 1)$
    $= 24 \times 20 - 24 \times 1$
    $= 480 - 24$
    $= 456$

3. (a) 475   (b) 608   (c) 1247   (d) 725   (e) 1755   (f) 2457

4. (a) 525   (b) 3875   (c) 6975   (d) 1025   (e) 11 475   (f) 7750

5. (a) 600   (b) 1680   (c) 1485   (d) 6720   (e) 3870   (f) 1820

6.　(a) 12　　(b) 45　　(c) 36　　(d) 30　　(e) 35　　(f) 42

7.　(a) 28　　(b) 28　　(c) 18　　(d)60　　(e) 315　　(f) 110

8.　(a) 6　　(b) 14　　(c) 14　　(d) Cannot do　　(e) 42　　(f) Cannot do

Exercise 2.11 : Summary exercise

1.　(a) 226-No　(b) 234-Yes　(c) 1434-Yes　(d) 132-Yes　(e) 231-No　(f) 9000-Yes

2.　(a) 9000　　(b) 234, 9000　(c) 231

3.　(a) 1, 2, 4, 8, 16, 32, 64
　　(b) 1, 2, 3, 4, 6, 8, 12, 24
　　(c) 1, 2, 3, 4, 5, 6, 10, 12, 15, 20, 25, 30, 50, 60, 75, 100, 150, 300

4.　(a) 7　　　　(d) 4 or 25
　　(b) 4　　　　(e) 4
　　(c) 32　　　(f) 10

5.　(a) $2^4 \times 3$　　(b) $2^2 \times 7^2$　　(c) $3^2 \times 5 \times 7$

6.　(a) 108　　(b) 200　　(c) 300

7.　4

8.　168

9.

The 7th triangle number will have a value of 28

10.　(a) Me £250, my brother £125 and my sister £375
　　(b) 17 m

End of chapter 2 activity: The number game
Practical

1.　2
2.　6
3.　49
4.　73
5.　7

6.　96
7.　55
8.　6 or 12
9.　31
10.　36

Chapter 3: Fractions

Exercise 3.1

1. (a) $\frac{3}{4} = \frac{9}{12}$ (b) $\frac{2}{7} = \frac{4}{14}$ (c) $\frac{4}{9} = \frac{12}{27}$ (d) $\frac{5}{6} = \frac{15}{18}$

2. (a) $\frac{5}{6}$ (b) $\frac{5}{6}$ (c) $\frac{1}{6}$ (d) $\frac{1}{4}$ (e) $\frac{3}{5}$

3. Check the pupils' drawings reflect the following fractions:

    (a) $\frac{7}{30}$ (b) $\frac{4}{15}$ (c) $\frac{5}{6}$ (d) $\frac{1}{10}$

4. (a) $\frac{1}{2}$ (e) $\frac{7}{100}$

    (b) $\frac{2}{5}$ (f) $\frac{9}{25}$

    (c) $\frac{2}{15}$ (g) $\frac{5}{16}$

    (d) $\frac{7}{20}$ (h) $\frac{3}{8}$

5. $\frac{3}{8} = \frac{15}{40}$ and $\frac{2}{5} = \frac{16}{40}$ $\frac{2}{5}$ is larger

6. (a) $\frac{5}{8}$ (b) $\frac{3}{4}$ (c) $\frac{7}{8}$ (d) $\frac{3}{7}$ (e) $\frac{4}{9}$ (f) $\frac{3}{5}$

7. $\frac{1}{16}$

8. $\frac{1}{5}$

9. $\frac{4}{15}$

10. $\frac{13}{48}$

11. $\frac{7}{15}$

12. $\frac{13}{36}$ including the 4 in his pocket!

Exercise 3.2

1. (a) 0.1   (b) 0.3   (c) 0.7   (d) 0.9

2. (a) 1%   (b) 43%   (c) 70%   (d) 90%

3. (a) (i) 0.2   (ii) $\frac{1}{5}$

    (b) (i) 0.4   (ii) $\frac{2}{5}$

(c) (i) 0.6   (ii) $\frac{3}{5}$

(d) (i) 0.8   (ii) $\frac{4}{5}$

4.   (a) (i) 25%   (ii) $\frac{1}{4}$

     (b) (i) 45%   (ii) $\frac{9}{20}$

     (c) (i) 65%   (ii) $\frac{13}{20}$

     (d) (i) 95%   (ii) $\frac{19}{20}$

5.   (a) (i) 0.375 (ii) 37.5%

     (b) (i) 0.625 (ii) 62.5%

     (c) (i) 0.875 (ii) 87.5%

6.   Check pupils have used a calculator to check all their fractions to decimal answers above.

7.   (a) $0.1\dot{6}$ (b) $0.\dot{6}$ (c) $0.8\dot{3}$ (d) $0.\dot{1}$

Exercise 3.3

1.   (a) $\frac{7}{4}$ (b) $\frac{17}{5}$ (c) $\frac{15}{7}$ (d) $\frac{34}{5}$ (e) $\frac{103}{10}$ (f) $\frac{76}{9}$

     (g) $\frac{52}{7}$ (h) $\frac{62}{5}$ (i) $\frac{55}{12}$ (j) $\frac{63}{4}$ (k) $\frac{82}{9}$ (l) $\frac{65}{12}$

2.   (a) $3\frac{1}{4}$ (b) $3\frac{1}{2}$ (c) $2\frac{1}{9}$ (d) 6   (e) $7\frac{3}{4}$ (f) $7\frac{7}{11}$

     (g) $2\frac{7}{8}$ (h) $2\frac{9}{10}$ (i) $13\frac{1}{2}$ (j) $3\frac{1}{4}$ (k) $20\frac{1}{5}$ (l) 5

Exercise 3.4

1. $\frac{13}{20}$ 4. $1\frac{13}{20}$ 7. $1\frac{7}{12}$

2. $\frac{26}{35}$ 5. $\frac{26}{45}$ 8. $1\frac{2}{15}$

3. $\frac{13}{15}$ 6. $\frac{27}{40}$ 9. $\frac{19}{24}$

10. $4\frac{13}{15}$ 14. $8\frac{7}{16}$ 18. $4\frac{7}{15}$

11. $5\frac{26}{35}$ 15. $4\frac{14}{15}$ 19. $7\frac{7}{12}$

12. $5\frac{21}{40}$ 16. $10\frac{1}{24}$ 20. $8\frac{3}{4}$

13. $9\frac{16}{45}$ 17. $6\frac{37}{40}$ 21. $7\frac{5}{12}$

Exercise 3.5

1. $\frac{2}{15}$

2. $\frac{5}{12}$

3. $\frac{23}{42}$

4. $\frac{1}{24}$

5. $\frac{1}{6}$

6. $\frac{23}{60}$

7. $\frac{9}{40}$

8. $\frac{3}{28}$

9. $\frac{1}{24}$

10. $2\frac{6}{35}$

11. $3\frac{8}{21}$

12. $3\frac{7}{15}$

13. $3\frac{8}{45}$

14. $4\frac{1}{9}$

15. $1\frac{9}{28}$

16. $4\frac{4}{9}$

17. $3\frac{1}{12}$

18. $4\frac{5}{24}$

19. $\frac{11}{15}$

20. $2\frac{39}{49}$

21. $\frac{8}{15}$

22. $1\frac{7}{8}$

23. $2\frac{22}{35}$

24. $\frac{7}{10}$

25. $\frac{11}{24}$

26. $1\frac{13}{21}$

27. $\frac{5}{12}$

28. $1\frac{5}{18}$

29. $\frac{15}{28}$

30. $3\frac{13}{24}$

Exercise 3.6

1. $\frac{1}{6}$

2. My friend

3. $\frac{1}{7}$

4. $2\frac{2}{3}$ metres

5. $\frac{7}{20}$

6. $4\frac{17}{20}$

7. Both equal $1\frac{1}{10}$

8. $4\frac{2}{5}$

Exercise 3.7

1.	4	**5.**	20.25 or $20\frac{1}{4}$
2.	5	**6.**	9.25 or $9\frac{1}{4}$
3.	13	**7.**	36
4.	14	**8.**	48

9. 60 cm
10. 40 minutes
11. 750 grams
12. 1 km and 875 m

13.	180	**20.**	235
14.	75	**21.**	117
15.	15	**22.**	49
16.	20	**23.**	65
17.	187	**24.**	84
18.	130	**25.**	56
19.	400.5 or $400\frac{1}{2}$	**26.**	45

Exercise 3.8

1.	$\frac{3}{5}$	**6.**	$\frac{1}{3}$	**11.**	$\frac{8}{21}$
2.	$\frac{3}{4}$	**7.**	$\frac{4}{15}$	**12.**	$\frac{1}{12}$
3.	$\frac{3}{18}$	**8.**	$\frac{2}{5}$	**13.**	$\frac{1}{4}$
4.	$\frac{4}{21}$	**9.**	$\frac{8}{15}$	**14.**	$\frac{160}{189}$
5.	$\frac{8}{9}$	**10.**	$\frac{8}{35}$	**15.**	$\frac{27}{50}$

16.	$\frac{8}{15}$	**19.**	$\frac{4}{9}$	**22.**	$\frac{2}{9}$
17.	$\frac{1}{2}$	**20.**	$\frac{1}{15}$	**23.**	$\frac{16}{39}$
18.	$\frac{8}{11}$	**21.**	$\frac{16}{165}$	**24.**	$\frac{1}{6}$

25.	$\frac{1}{6}$	**27.**	$\frac{2}{39}$
26.	$\frac{1}{5}$	**28.**	$\frac{231}{1024}$

Exercise 3.9

Various equivalent answers to:

1. $\frac{1}{4}$ of 8
2. $6 \div 2$
3. $10 \times \frac{3}{5}$
4. $9 \div 4$
5. $6 \times \frac{2}{3}$
6. $10 \div 3$
7. $\frac{1}{5}$ of 16
8. 25 % of 12
9. 0.3×3

But note that **9** is not equal to a third of the amount! $\frac{10}{3} = 3\frac{1}{3}$ is a third of 10 and $\frac{1}{3}$ of 10 = $3\frac{1}{3}$

Exercise 3.10

1. $\frac{7}{10}$
2. $\frac{6}{7}$
3. $\frac{3}{4}$
4. $1\frac{1}{3}$
5. $1\frac{1}{20}$
6. $1\frac{1}{2}$
7. $1\frac{1}{54}$
8. $1\frac{1}{6}$
9. $\frac{9}{10}$
10. $1\frac{1}{2}$
11. $1\frac{1}{2}$
12. $1\frac{1}{7}$

13. $\frac{64}{75}$
14. $1\frac{1}{4}$
15. $1\frac{1}{2}$
16. $\frac{7}{10}$
17. $\frac{1}{2}$
18. $1\frac{1}{2}$
19. 3
20. $\frac{3}{7}$
21. $1\frac{4}{5}$
22. $1\frac{1}{4}$
23. $\frac{1}{6}$
24. $2\frac{2}{7}$

Exercise 3.11: Mixed operations

Check pupils have used the BIDMAS rule to calculate the answers to these.

1. $\frac{17}{24}$
2. $\frac{7}{12}$
3. $1\frac{5}{8}$
4. $\frac{7}{16}$
5. $\frac{1}{12}$
6. 1
7. $\frac{1}{4}$
8. $1\frac{11}{21}$
9. $1\frac{17}{21}$
10. $\frac{7}{16}$

Exercise 3.12

1. 45 miles

2. 250 km distance

3. £1.20

4. $2\frac{1}{4}$m

5. $5\frac{1}{8}$ metres

6. One quarter

7. 10 minutes

8. $\frac{5}{6}$

9. 3

10. $\frac{1}{4}$

Exercise 3.13: Extension questions

1. $2\frac{3}{10}$

2. $\frac{5}{7}$

3. $3\frac{1}{36}$

4. $4\frac{17}{20}$

5. 1

6. $4\frac{1}{16}$

7. $1\frac{3}{4}$

8. $1\frac{11}{20}$

9. $1\frac{1}{5}$

10. $3\frac{5}{19}$

11. $\frac{51}{65}$

12. $\frac{49}{60}$

13. $\frac{25}{32}$

14. $\frac{137}{160}$

15. (a) $2\frac{83}{140}$ (b) He will not have one; the sum never quite gets to 2

16. (a) $\frac{1}{5}$ (b) $\frac{1}{20}$ (c) $10\frac{1}{2}$ (d) $\frac{21}{40}$

Exercise 3.14: Summary exercise

1. (a) $\frac{9}{30} = \frac{3}{10}$ (b) $\frac{8}{30} = \frac{4}{15}$

2.

Fraction	Decimal	Percentage
$\frac{3}{4}$	0.75	75%
$\frac{65}{100} = \frac{13}{20}$	0.65	65%
$\frac{4}{5}$	0.8	80%
$\frac{1}{8}$	0.125	12.5%

3. (a) $1\frac{7}{12}$ (b) $6\frac{11}{35}$ **4.** (a) $\frac{9}{40}$ (b) $2\frac{1}{24}$

5. 50

6. 1125 grams

7. (a) $\frac{3}{8}$ (b) $\frac{21}{64}$ **8.** (a) $\frac{1}{6}$ (b) $3\frac{1}{3}$

9. (d) $4 \div 25$

10. $1\frac{7}{12}$

11. $\frac{7}{12}$

12. $23\frac{3}{4}$ **13.** $\frac{45}{64}$

End of chapter 3 activity: 'Equivalent fraction' dominoes

Practical work

Chapter 4: Probability

Exercise 4.1

1.   Check pupils' answers for:
      (a) An event that is impossible.
      (b) An event that is possible.
      (c) An event that has an even chance of happening.
      (d) An event that is probable.
      (e) An event that is certain.

2.   (a) Check pupils' answers.
      (b) 25% or equivalent.

3.   (a) Check pupils' answers.
      (b) 0.9 or equivalent.

4.   (a) Thursday
      (b) Even chance on Tuesday
      (c) Probable on Wednesday

5.   Check pupils' answers; B should be an even chance.

6.   B: I throw a three
      C: I throw a square number
      A: I throw an odd number
      E: I throw less than five
      D: I throw at least two

Exercise 4.2

1.   (a) $\frac{1}{2}$ (b) $\frac{1}{6}$ (c) $\frac{1}{3}$ (d) $\frac{5}{6}$ (e) $\frac{2}{3}$

2.   (a) $\frac{1}{4}$ (b) $\frac{1}{13}$ (c) $\frac{3}{13}$ (d) $\frac{1}{26}$ (e) $\frac{1}{2}$

3. $\frac{4}{11}$

4.   (a) $\frac{1}{8}$ (b) $\frac{1}{2}$ (c) $\frac{1}{2}$ (d) $\frac{1}{4}$ (e) $\frac{1}{4}$

5.   (a) $\frac{1}{5}$ (b) $\frac{2}{5}$ (c) $\frac{3}{5}$ (d) $\frac{2}{5}$

6.   (a) $\frac{1}{5}$ (b) $\frac{3}{5}$ (c) $\frac{2}{5}$

Exercise 4.3

1.   (a) $\frac{1}{2}$ (b) $\frac{2}{5}$ (c) $\frac{3}{5}$ (d) $\frac{7}{10}$ (e) $\frac{9}{10}$ (f) $\frac{7}{20}$ (g) $\frac{3}{4}$

2.   (a) $\frac{1}{13}$ (b) $\frac{8}{13}$ (c) $\frac{12}{13}$ (d) $\frac{10}{13}$

3.   (a) $\frac{1}{2}$ (b) $\frac{1}{2}$ (c) $\frac{3}{8}$ (d) $\frac{1}{2}$ (e) $\frac{1}{4}$ (f) 1

4.   (a) $\frac{1}{5}$ (b) $\frac{3}{10}$ (c) $\frac{4}{5}$ (d) $\frac{7}{20}$ (e) 0

Exercise 4.4

1.   (a) $\frac{5}{19}$ (b) $\frac{3}{19}$

2.   (a) $\frac{3}{13}$ (b) $\frac{11}{26}$ (c) $\frac{9}{26}$ (d) $\frac{1}{5}$ (e) $\frac{11}{25}$

3.   (a) $\frac{1}{5}$ (b) $\frac{60}{150} = \frac{2}{5}$

4.   (a) $\frac{3}{46}$ (b) $\frac{2}{45}$

5.   (a) $\frac{1}{6}$ (b) $\frac{1}{6}$ (c) $\frac{1}{6}$ (d) $\frac{1}{6}$ (e) If she had rolled a 3, none of the answers would be different. If she had rolled a 1, (d) would be 0.

Exercise 4.5

1.

		First die					
		1	2	3	4	5	6
Second die	1	(1,1)	(2,1)	(3,1)	(4,1)	(5,1)	(6,1)
	2	(1,2)	(2,2)	(3,2)	(4,2)	(5,2)	(6,2)
	3	(1,3)	(2,3)	(3,3)	(4,3)	(5,3)	(6,3)
	4	(1,4)	(2,4)	(3,4)	(4,4)	(5,4)	(6,4)
	5	(1,5)	(2,5)	(3,5)	(4,5)	(5,5)	(6,5)
	6	(1,6)	(2,6)	(3,6)	(4,6)	(5,6)	(6,6)

(a) $\frac{1}{36}$ (e) $\frac{21}{36} = \frac{7}{12}$

(b) $\frac{1}{6}$ (f) $\frac{30}{36} = \frac{5}{6}$

(c) $\frac{1}{6}$ (g) $\frac{11}{36}$

(d) $\frac{1}{12}$

2.

		Coloured die					
		B	B	B	R	R	Y
Numbered die	1	(B,1)	(B,1)	(B,1)	(R,1)	(R,1)	(Y,1)
	2	(B,2)	(B,2)	(B,2)	(R,2)	(R,2)	(Y,2)
	3	(B,3)	(B,3)	(B,3)	(R,3)	(R,3)	(Y,3)
	4	(B,4)	(B,4)	(B,4)	(R,4)	(R,4)	(Y,4)
	5	(B,5)	(B,5)	(B,5)	(R,5)	(R,5)	(Y,5)
	6	(B,6)	(B,6)	(B,6)	(R,6)	(R,6)	(Y,6)

(a) $\frac{1}{12}$ (b) $\frac{1}{36}$ (c) $\frac{1}{3}$ (d) $\frac{1}{6}$

3.

		4-sided spinner			
		y	r	g	b
5-sided spinner	A	(y,A)	(r,A)	(g,A)	(b,A)
	B	(y,B)	(r,B)	(g,B)	(b,B)
	C	(y,C)	(r,C)	(g,C)	(b,C)
	D	(y,D)	(r,D)	(g,D)	(b,D)
	E	(y,E)	(r,E)	(g,E)	(b,E)

(a) $\frac{1}{4}$ (b) $\frac{1}{20}$

4.

		First die					
		1	2	3	4	5	6
Second die	1	(1,1)	(2,1)	(3,1)	(4,1)	(5,1)	(6,1)
	1	(1,1)	(2,1)	(3,1)	(4,1)	(5,1)	(6,1)
	2	(1,2)	(2,2)	(3,2)	(4,2)	(5,2)	(6,2)
	2	(1,2)	(2,2)	(3,2)	(4,2)	(5,2)	(6,2)
	3	(1,3)	(2,3)	(3,3)	(4,3)	(5,3)	(6,3)
	4	(1,4)	(2,4)	(3,4)	(4,4)	(5,4)	(6,4)

(a) $\frac{1}{18}$ (d) $\frac{1}{6}$

(b) $\frac{1}{6}$ (e) $\frac{1}{6}$

(c) 0   (f) $\frac{1}{12}$

Exercise 4.6: Extension questions

1. (a) (i) $\frac{1}{8}$ (ii) $\frac{1}{4}$ (iii) $\frac{1}{2}$ (b) $\frac{1}{2}$

2. (a) (i) $\frac{1}{5}$ (ii) $\frac{2}{5}$ (iii) $\frac{3}{5}$

   (b) (i) $\frac{1}{4}$ (ii) $\frac{5}{12}$ (iii) $\frac{7}{12}$

   (c) Spinning A twice $\frac{8}{25}$, spinning B twice $\frac{49}{144}$, spinning A and B together.
   Therefore spin both together.

3. (a) (i) $\frac{18}{100} = \frac{9}{50}$ about $\frac{1}{5}$ (ii) $\frac{69}{100}$ about $\frac{7}{10}$ (iii) $\frac{31}{100}$ about $\frac{3}{10}$ (iv) $\frac{13}{100}$ about $\frac{1}{10}$

   (b) Not exactly the same but if the tests are 'fair' then the results would be approximately the same.

   (c)

		Die				
	1	2	3	4	5	6
Stay (S)	(1,S)	(2,S)	(3,S)	(4,S)	(5,S)	(6,S)
Right (R)	(1,R)	(2,R)	(3,R)	(4,R)	(5,R)	(6,R)
Left (L)	(1,L)	(2,L)	(3,L)	(4,L)	(5,L)	(6,L)
Forward (F)	(1,F)	(2,F)	(3,F)	(4,F)	(5,F)	(6,F)
Back (B)	(1,B)	(2,B)	(3,B)	(4,B)	(5,B)	(6,B)

   (d) No, because the probabilities of S, R, L, F and B are not equal.

   Probability is $\frac{1}{6} \times \frac{8}{100} \rightarrow \frac{1}{75}$ approximately.

Exercise 4.7: Summary exercise

1. Check pupils' answers.

2. (a) $\frac{4}{11}$ (b) $\frac{7}{11}$ (c) $\frac{1}{11}$ (d) $\frac{3}{11}$

3. (a) $\frac{1}{13}$ (b) $\frac{5}{13}$ (c) $\frac{3}{26}$ (d) $\frac{1}{13}$ (e) $\frac{1}{4}$ (f) $\frac{4}{13}$

4. (a) $\frac{1}{6}$ (b) $\frac{1}{2}$ (c) $\frac{5}{6}$

5.

Coin		Dice					
		1	2	3	4	5	6
	H	(1,H)	(2,H)	(3,H)	(4,H)	(5,H)	(6,H)
	T	(1,T)	(2,T)	(3,T)	(4,T)	(5,T)	(6,T)

(a) $\frac{1}{4}$ (b) $\frac{1}{6}$ (c) $\frac{1}{2}$ (d) 0

6.

Second die		First die					
		1	1	2	2	3	3
	1	(1,1)	(1,1)	(2,1)	(2,1)	(3,1)	(3,1)
	1	(1,1)	(1,1)	(2,1)	(2,1)	(3,1)	(3,1)
	2	(1,2)	(1,2)	(2,2)	(2,2)	(3,2)	(3,2)
	2	(1,2)	(1,2)	(2,2)	(2,2)	(3,2)	(3,2)
	2	(1,2)	(1,2)	(2,2)	(2,2)	(3,2)	(3,2)
	3	(1,3)	(1,3)	(2,3)	(2,3)	(3,3)	(3,3)

(a) $\frac{1}{18}$ (b) $\frac{1}{3}$ (c) $\frac{1}{3}$ (d) $\frac{10}{36} = \frac{5}{18}$ (e) 2, 3, 4, 5, 6 (f) 4

7. (a) $\frac{1}{7}$ (b) $\frac{2}{7}$ (c) $\frac{1}{12}$ (d) $\frac{4}{12} = \frac{1}{3}$

End of chapter 4 activity: Designing a board game

A good way to introduce this project would be to play some different games, using dice, spinners and cards, or even pigs!

Chapter 5: Handling data

There is no reason why a calculator should not be used throughout this chapter; however use of the statistical functions on a scientific calculator should be treated with some discretion. More able pupils and those that finish quickly will probably enjoy checking their answers with these functions but other children can find them more confusing than useful.

Exercise 5.1

1. (a) Mean 3; Range 5 – 1 = 4

    (b) Mean 60; Range 95 – 21 = 74

    (c) Mean 4.93; Range 8.1 – 1.4 = 6.7

    (d) Mean 1461; Range 1672 – 1234 = 438

2. 67.5%

3. Both are 16

4. (a) Mean 1.4; Range 3 – 0 = 3

    (b) Mean 1.7; Range 4 – 0 = 4

5. 10y 10m

6. 378

7. 1265 grams

8. (a) 301 kg   (b) 340 kg   (c) 42.5 kg

9. (a) 1224   (b) 69%

10. (a) 183 years 9 months   (b) 11 years 7 months

Exercise 5.2

(Q4-6 are considerably harder than 1-3)

1. (a) Median 6; Mode 6

    (b) Median 2.5; Mode 3

    (c) Median 20; Mode 20

2. (a) Median 5; Mode 5

    (b) Median 16; Mode 13 and 18

    (c) Median 0.202; Mode 0.2 and 0.202

3. (a) Range 98 – 38 60;   Mean $55\frac{5}{6}$;   Median 46;   Mode 46

  (b) Range 5.2 – 4.2 1;   Mean 4.63;   Median 4.6;   Mode 4.2

  (c) Range 112 – 100 12;   Mean 107;   Median 107;   Mode 104 and 111

4. (a) Range $\frac{3}{4} - \frac{1}{8} = \frac{5}{8}$;   Mean $\frac{13}{32}$;   Median $\frac{7}{16}$;   Mode $\frac{1}{8}$ and $\frac{1}{2}$

  (b) Range $2\frac{3}{4} - 1\frac{3}{4} = 1$;   Mean $2\frac{1}{4}$;   Median $2\frac{1}{4}$;   Mode $2\frac{1}{4}$

  (c) Range $7\frac{1}{5} - 5\frac{2}{5} = 1\frac{4}{5}$;   Mean $6\frac{14}{25}$;   Median $= 6\frac{3}{4}$;   Mode $7\frac{1}{5}$

5. They are the same.

6. 4, 4, 4, 4, 6, 6, 6, 7, 7, 7

Exercise 5.3

Pupils can find the concept of working from a frequency table quite hard and Q3 should be explained carefully before they attempt it by themselves.

1. (a)

Mark	Tally	Frequency
16	IIII	4
17	III	3
18	III	3
19	III	3
20	III	3
21	II	2
22	II	2
23	I	1
24	II	2
25	I	1
Total		24

  (b) Range 25 – 16 = 9

  (c) Mean 19.5; Mode 16; Median 19

  (d) No one achieved less than 16! More people (1 more pupil) achieved more than the median mark than less than the median mark.

2. (a)

Heights	Tally	Frequency
12	I	1
13	II	2
14	III	3
15	ЖН I	6
16	III	3
17	II	2
18	I	1
Total		18

(b) 15

(c) 18 – 12 = 6

3. (a) 18 – 12 = 6   (b) 16

(c) (i) 20   (ii) 16 and 16   (iii) 16

(d) 305

(e) 15.25

4. (a) Range 25 – 17 = 8; Mode 22; Median 21.5; Mean 21.2

(b)

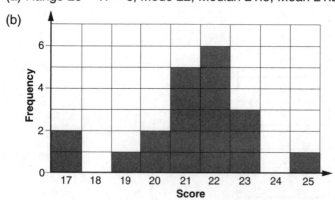

(c) Yes, but you need to work out the total number before you can calculate the mean.

5. (a) 7 – 1 = 6   (b) 3   (c) 3   (d) 3.73

6. (a) Car is the modal group.

Type of vehicle	Tally	Frequency
Car	ⅢⅠ ⅢⅠ ⅢⅠ ⅢⅠ Ⅲ	23
Van	ⅢⅠ Ⅱ	7
Lorry	Ⅰ	1
Motorbike	Ⅲ	3
Bicycle	ⅢⅠ	4
Total		38

(b) Because it is not appropriate for the data.

Exercise 5.4

1. (a)

No of brothers and sisters	Frequency	Calculation	Angle
0	9	$\frac{360}{36} \times 9$	90°
1	12	$\frac{360}{36} \times 12$	120°
2	9	$\frac{360}{36} \times 9$	90°
3	5	$\frac{360}{36} \times 5$	50°
4	1	$\frac{360}{36} \times 1$	10°
Total	36		360°

(b) **A pie chart to show the number of brothers and sisters in a year group**

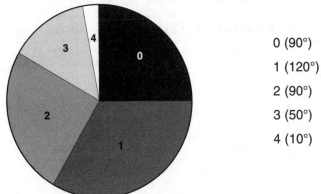

0 (90°)

1 (120°)

2 (90°)

3 (50°)

4 (10°)

2. (a) and (b)

No hours	Frequency	Calculation	Angle
0-2	1	$\frac{360}{30} \times 1$	12°
2-4	3	$\frac{360}{30} \times 3$	36°
4-6	5	$\frac{360}{30} \times 5$	60°
6-8	12	$\frac{360}{30} \times 12$	144°
8-10	6	$\frac{360}{30} \times 5$	72°
More than 10	3	$\frac{360}{30} \times 3$	36°
Total	30		360°

(c)   **A pie chart to show the number of hours spent watching television**

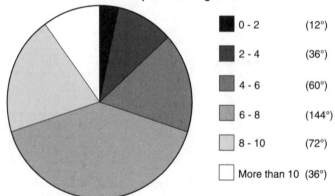

■	0 - 2	(12°)
■	2 - 4	(36°)
■	4 - 6	(60°)
■	6 - 8	(144°)
■	8 - 10	(72°)
□	More than 10	(36°)

3. (a) and (b)

Method	Frequency	Calculation	Angle
Walk	60	$\frac{360}{240} \times 60$	90°
School bus	48	$\frac{360}{240} \times 48$	72°
Car	96	$\frac{360}{240} \times 96$	144°
Public transport	36	$\frac{360}{240} \times 36$	54°
Total	240		360°

(c)

A pie chart to show how pupils come to school

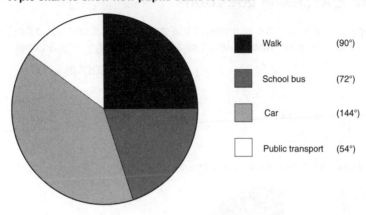

■	Walk	(90°)
▦	School bus	(72°)
▨	Car	(144°)
□	Public transport	(54°)

(d) $\frac{1}{4}$

4. (a) and (b)

Item	Frequency	Calculation	Angle
Yoghurt	10	$\frac{360}{72} \times 10$	50°
Apple	18	$\frac{360}{72} \times 18$	90°
Banana	8	$\frac{360}{72} \times 8$	40°
Chocolate bar	12	$\frac{360}{72} \times 12$	60°
Crisps	24	$\frac{360}{72} \times 24$	120°
Total	72		360°

(c)

A pie chart to show the lunch items bought by pupils for a school trip

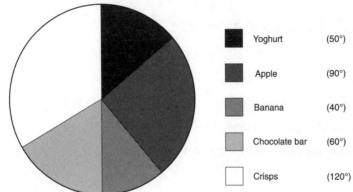

■	Yoghurt	(50°)
▦	Apple	(90°)
▨	Banana	(40°)
▨	Chocolate bar	(60°)
□	Crisps	(120°)

(d) $\frac{1}{3}$

Exercise 5.6: Extension questions

1. At first it appears as if you are estimating the fractions, but once you have the total of 48 in a class then the numbers must be whole numbers and there is only one answer.

    (a) $\frac{1}{3}$ (b) $\frac{1}{4}$ (c) $\frac{1}{4}$ (d) 48 (e) 2

2. (a) $\frac{2}{5}$ (b) 411

    (c)   **A pie chart to show how we come to school**

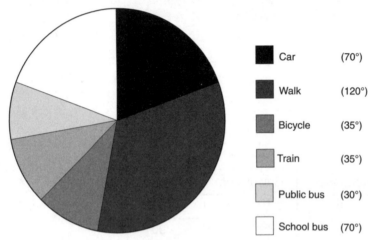

Car	(70°)
Walk	(120°)
Bicycle	(35°)
Train	(35°)
Public bus	(30°)
School bus	(70°)

3. (a) Europe (b) one tenth (c) one eighth (d) 100
4. Check pupils' own answers.

Exercise 5.7: Summary exercise

1. (a) 1.42 (b) 1.50 – 1.35 = 0.15
2. (a) 10y 11m (b) 11y 11m
3. (a) Mean $5\frac{1}{3}$; Median 5; Mode 4

    (b) Mean 1.9; Median 1.9; Mode 2.1

    (c) Mean 13.4; Median 13.5; Mode 14.1

4. (a)

Mark	Tally	Frequency
11	I	1
12	I	1
13	II	2
14	III	3
15	IIII	4
16	III	3
17	II	2
18	I	1
19	I	1
Total		18

(b) Mean 15; Mode 15; Median 15

(c) **A pie chart to show marks achieved in a recent mental arithmetic test**

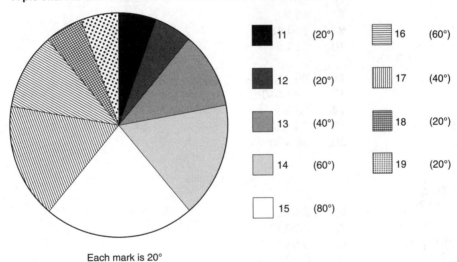

11 (20°)   16 (60°)

12 (20°)   17 (40°)

13 (40°)   18 (20°)

14 (60°)   19 (20°)

15 (80°)

Each mark is 20°

5. (a) 36   (b) 12   (c) 83   (d) 259   (e) 3   (f) 3.1 approx.

End of chapter 5 activity: A traffic survey

It may be that this is the time to work with the geography department on the mathematics requirement for the pupils' fieldwork.

Chapter 6: Working with decimals

Exercise 6.1

1. 17.5
2. 0.8
3. 10.15
4. 2.92
5. 21.13

6. 11.034
7. 18.194
8. 2.61
9. 8.811
10. 6.873

11. 25.724
12. 127.755
13. 438.357
14. 3.568
15. 16.34

16. 19.327
17. 0.031
18. 1.867
19. 92.966
20. 17.001

Exercise 6.2

1. 5.1
2. 1.8
3. 22.75
4. 80.45
5. 34.08

6. 66.42
7. 187.2
8. 46.9
9. 160.48
10. 126.54

11. 74.4
12. 672
13. 185.4
14. 1126.3
15. 2629.6

16. 20 115
17. 199 440
18. 284
19. 36 480
20. 38 430

Exercise 6.3

1. 0.28
2. 0.028
3. 0.000 28
4. 0.28
5. 0.4

6. 0.072
7. 0.0032
8. 0.612
9. 0.005 05
10. 0.06

11. 1.86
12. 1.584
13. 5.76
14. 0.348
15. 0.081

16. 0.536
17. 0.54
18. 0.3563
19. 0.0028
20. 5.463

21. 18.72
22. 3.6
23. 0.546
24. 41.48
25. 189.84

26. 1.1128
27. 0.4368
28. 0.728
29. 0.03 852
30. 6.048

Exercise 6.4

1.	(a) 39.01	(b) 390.1	(c) 3901
2.	(a)19.72	(b) 197.2	(c) 1972
3.	(a) 28.35	(b) 2835	(c) 283.5
4.	(a) 154.8	(b) 1548	(c) 15 480
5.	(a) 75.632	(b) 7563.2	(c) 75 632

Exercise 6.5

1.	0.6	**6.**	0.007	**11.**	0.3
2.	0.05	**7.**	0.9	**12.**	0.7
3.	0.005	**8.**	0.6	**13.**	0.007
4.	0.2	**9.**	0.07	**14.**	0.12
5.	0.11	**10.**	0.0011	**15.**	0.012

Exercise 6.6

1.	4.6	**6.**	0.95
2.	0.48	**7.**	0.056
3.	0.069	**8.**	8.4
4.	0.45	**9.**	0.036
5.	0.58	**10.**	0.0054

Exercise 6.7

1.	1.25	**6.**	0.3375	**11.**	0.1325
2.	0.225	**7.**	0.045	**12.**	3.025
3.	0.005	**8.**	0.26	**13.**	1.25
4.	0.005	**9.**	0.154	**14.**	0.0675
5.	0.2575	**10.**	0.002 25	**15.**	0.775

Exercise 6.8

1.	40	**6.**	4
2.	0.4	**7.**	80
3.	4	**8.**	0.02
4.	300	**9.**	700
5.	0.4	**10.**	30 000

11.	1.75	**16.**	0.7
12.	0.008	**17.**	900
13.	4	**18.**	0.004
14.	80	**19.**	800
15.	400	**20.**	0.0002

Exercise 6.9

1.	(a) 580	(b) 1600	(c) 5800
2.	(a) 360	(b) 850	(c) 36
3.	(a) 56	(b) 29	(c) 5.6
4.	(a) 0.79	(b) 0.248	(c) 79 000
5.	(a) 245	(b) 1.24	(c) 245

Exercise 6.10

1.	(a) 0.25 m	(b) 0.48 m	(c) 5 300 m	(d) 2.58 m
2.	(a) 25 000 g	(b) 3.750 g	(c) 625 g	(d) 3 600 000 g
3.	(a) 0. 220 l	(b) 3.634 l	(c) 0.028 l	(d) 0.005 l
4.	(a) 2.4 cm	(b) 270 000 cm	(c) 3500 cm	(d) 7 cm
5	(a) 0.35 kg	(b) 4 500 kg	(c) 0.000 025 kg	(d) 0.0075 kg
6.	(a) 1400 ml	(b) 350 ml	(c) 450 ml	(d) 7 ml
7.	(a) 32 mm	(b) 4500 mm	(c) 700 mm	(d) 400 000 mm
8.	(a) 3200 mg	(b) 5500 mg	(c) 165 000 mg	(d) 60 000 mg
9.	(a) 0.0035 km	(b) 4.050 km	(c) 3.2 km	

Exercise 6.11

1.	1178.5 cm	4.	3 l
2.	5200.375 g	5.	250 m
3.	632.75 m	6.	475 000 g

7.	9 metres
8.	0.9 kg (or 900 g)
9.	16
10.	43.88 centimetres
11.	1450 g or 1.45 kg
12.	125 ml

Exercise 6.12: Extension questions

1.	9	5.	11.5
2.	13	6.	26
3.	7	7.	113
4.	5	8.	21

Exercise 6.13: Summary exercise

1.   (a) 19.656   (b) 2.725
2.   (a) 0.2   (b) 0.024   (c) 0.04
3.   (a) 0.2   (b) 60   (c) 400
4.   (a) 0.95   (b) 5.985
5.   0.032
6.   (a) 4.704   (b) 470.4   (c) 0.84   (d) 56
7.   (a) 1.3 g = 1300 mg   (c) 7.2 km = 7200 m
    (b) 53 mm = 0.053 m   (d) 0.072 ml = 0.000 072 l
8.   (a) 903.6 cm   (b) 4256.765 kg   (c) 625 ml   (d) 0.0012 kg
9.   250 ml
10. 2100.045 g
11. 550 m

End of chapter 6 activity: Imperial units

1-4   Check pupils' own results.

5.   (a) Connie was going shopping for her mother. She walked **3.2 km** into the village. Connie bought **0.9 kg** of potatoes and **225 g** of mushrooms.

    (b) Connie walked **90 m** down the road to the Haberdashers shop. Connie then bought **270 cm (2.7 m)** of blue ribbon and **1.5 m** of knicker elastic.

    (c) Connie was tired and the shopping was heavy and so she stopped at the sweet shop and bought **100 g (112.5 g)** of wine gums.

6.   (a) Digby bicycled **2.5 miles** to the shops where he bought a **4.4 lb** weight and 6 weights of **10 oz** ($10\frac{2}{3}$ **oz) (10.6 oz)**

    (b) Digby also bought **650 feet** of fishing twine and **1 foot 8 inches** of string.

    (c) Digby was thirsty and so he also bought a **pint (0.875 pints)** bottle of water.

7.   Check pupils' own stories.

Chapter 7: Algebra 1 – Expressions and formulae

Exercise 7.1

1. $3a$
2. $5x$
3. $2m$
4. $2p + 2q$
5. $7y$

6. $s - 2t$
7. $2d$
8. $2x$
9. $2a + 10$
10. $-2c$

11. $6ab$
12. $4q - 2p$
13. $2m - n$
14. $20xy$
15. $\frac{4x}{y}$

16. $6a + 2b$
17. $-2m - 1$
18. $\frac{3m}{n}$
19. $10pq$
20. $6a$

Exercise 7.2

1. (a) x^2 (b) $2x$ (c) $2x$ (d) $4x$
2. (a) $3x$ (b) $3x$ (c) x^3 (d) $9x$
3. (a) $4x$ (b) x^4 (c) $4x^2$
4. (a) ax (b) ax^2 (c) a^2x (d) a^2x^2
5. (a) b^2 (b) $2b^2$ (c) $2ab$ (d) a^2b^2
6. (a) $xy + x$ (b) $xy + x^2$ (c) $2xy$ (d) $3x^2$

7. (a) $2ab + a^2$ (b) $3a^2$
8. (a) $2ab + ab^2$ (b) $5ab$
9. (a) $stu + st^2$ (b) st^2
10. (a) $2x^2y$ (b) $3x^2y - xy^2$

Exercise 7.3

1. a^6
2. $6a^6$
3. $3b + b^2 + 2b^3$
4. $6b^2$
5. $6a^4b^4$
6. $8x^2y$
7. $3xy + x^2y$
8. $4xy + x^2y - xy^2$
9. $12a^3b^2c^2$
10. $2bc + a^2b + 4ac$

Exercise 7.4

1. $3ab$
2. $2ab$
3. $\dfrac{ab}{2}$
4. $6b$
5. $6a$
6. $\dfrac{b}{2}$
7. $2a$
8. 6
9. 1
10. $\dfrac{2}{5}$

11. $\dfrac{xy}{2}$
12. $2p$
13. $\dfrac{2n}{3}$
14. $\dfrac{a}{2}$
15. $\dfrac{2m}{3}$
16. $5x$
17. $2a$
18. $3x$
19. 3
20. $\dfrac{4a}{b}$

Exercise 7.5

1. 9
2. 12
3. 36
4. $9b^2$
5. $3a^2$
6. $16x^2$
7. x^4
8. $6b^3$
9. $24b^3$
10. $54b^3$

Exercise 7.6

1.	$7x$	6.	0
2.	a^3	7.	$3a^3$
3.	$2ax$	8.	$6y^2$
4.	$2xy$	9.	b
5.	$4b^2$	10.	b

11.	$4b$	16.	$y - 2x$
12.	1	17.	$11 - 9x$
13.	$\dfrac{3a}{2}$	18.	$\dfrac{3b}{2}$
14.	$\dfrac{a}{3}$	19.	$18ab^2c$
15.	$27b^2$	20.	$3c$

Exercise 7.7

1.	-10	6.	4
2.	-3	7.	-8
3.	-14	8.	0
4.	-8	9.	-4
5.	-5	10.	3

11.	-15	16.	-9
12.	-4	17.	-15
13.	-18	18.	2
14.	-21	19.	-11
15.	22	20.	-5

Exercise 7.8

1.	12	6.	18
2.	−20	7.	24
3.	32	8.	−32
4.	−30	9.	−20
5.	15	10.	12

11.	54	16.	−25
12.	−16	17.	−21
13.	24	18.	−16
14.	−36	19.	−40
15.	−36	20.	56

Exercise 7.9

1.	2	6.	3
2.	−3	7.	4
3.	−4	8.	9
4.	−5	9.	−8
5.	−4	10.	−5

11.	−8	16.	12
12.	5	17.	−5
13.	−4	18.	−5
14.	−4	19.	2
15.	−9	20.	10

Exercise 7.10: Mixed examples

1.	−16	6.	−7
2.	3	7.	3
3.	−9	8.	6
4.	−7	9.	18
5.	1	10.	−5

11.	−72	**16.**	8
12.	3	**17.**	36
13.	−10	**18.**	24
14.	24	**19.**	36
15.	−10	**20.**	4

21.	4	**26.**	−6
22.	−13	**27.**	−5
23.	12	**28.**	−27
24.	0	**29.**	−14
25.	−9	**30.**	1

Exercise 7.11

1.	(a) 2	(b) 8	(c) 10	(d) 7
2.	(a) −6	(b) 9	(c) 18	(d) 36
3.	(a) 8	(b) 25	(c) 26	(d) 20
4.	(a) 0	(b) 0	(c) 4	(d) 15
5.	(a) 3	(b) 1	(c) 8	(d) 2
6.	(a) 6	(b) −2	(c) −8	(d) −2
7.	(a) 1	(b) 13	(c) 0	(d) −6
8.	(a) 13	(b) −5	(c) 16	(d) 0
9.	(a) 0	(b) −128	(c) −4	
10.	(a) 0	(b) 30	(c) 14	
11.	(a) 0.9	(b) 27.9	(c) 15.75	
12.	(a) 150	(b) 12.5	(c) 100	

Exercise 7.12: Substituting into formulae

1.	(a) 16	(b) 300	(c) 4	(d) 2	(e) 15
2.	(a) 10	(b) 4000	(c) 0.3	(d) 5	(e) 10
3.	(a) 36	(b) 1400	(c) 0.765	(d) 1	(e) 30
4.	(a) 36	(b) 0	(c) 5	(d) 12	

Exercise 7.13: Writing formulae

1. $S = x + y$

2. $L = s - t$

3. $C = mn$

4. $C = ct + t(c - 1)$ or $t(2c - 1)$

5. $P = 7x + y (50 - x)$

6. $b = 24 - g - s$

7. (a) $C_1 = xy$

    (b) $C_2 = \dfrac{xy}{100}$

8. $T = 160 - a - b$ or $T = \dfrac{160 - (a + b)}{100}$

9. $F = 500 - mp$

10. (a) $C_1 = 150 + 4.5p$ (b) $C_2 = \dfrac{150 + 4.5p}{p}$

11. (a) $P = 2p + q$ (b) $P = q + 2 (24 - p - q) = 48 - 2p - q$

12. $T = 1 + x + xy + xyz$

Exercise 7.14: Shape formulae

1. (a) $x = a + b$ (b) $x = a - b$ (c) $x = b - a$

2. (a) $x = a + b + c$ (b) $x = a - b - c$

    (c) $x = b - a - c$ (d) $x = a + b - c$

3. (a) $Area = gh$ (b) $Perimeter = 2g + 2h$ or $2 (g + h)$

4. (a) $P = 10x + 10y$ (b) $A = 16xy$

5. (a) $P = 6a + 6b$ (b) $A = 5ab$

6. (a) $P = 20a + 6b$ (b) $A = 14ab$

7. (a) $P = 10m + 16n$ (b) $A = 16mn$

8. Check pupils have drawn a shape with an area of $20ab$, and check their formula for its perimeter.

9. Check pupils have drawn a shape with a perimeter of $8a + 10b$, and check their formula for its area.

Exercise 7.15: Extension questions – Harder substitution

1. (a) $1\frac{1}{30}$ (b) $1\frac{7}{30}$ (c) $\frac{289}{900}$ (d) $9\frac{1}{36}$ (e) $\frac{4}{15}$ (f) $\frac{3}{20}$

2. (a) $\frac{79}{150}$ (b) $\frac{9}{40}$ (c) $\frac{25}{27}$ (d) $\frac{10}{51}$ (e) $1\frac{21}{55}$ (f) $\frac{19}{30}$

3. (a) 0.5   (b) 0.32   (c) 0.89   (d) 5   (e) 0.064   (f) $\frac{45}{99}$ or $0.\dot{4}\dot{5}$

Exercise 7.16: Summary exercise

1. (a) $3m$ (b) $2a - b$

2. (a) $2b^2$ (b) $2b^6$

3. (a) $3b$ (c) p
   (b) $\frac{y}{6}$ (d) $8n^2$

4. (a) $9a^2$ (b) $6a^2$

5. (a) 5   (d) 8   (g) 1
   (b) −11   (e) −9   (h) −24
   (c) −7   (f) −24   (i) 2

6. (a) (i) 10   (ii) 25   (iii) 50   (iv) 100
   (b) (i) −6   (ii) 9   (iii) 18   (iv) 36

7. (a) −4   (b) 8   (c) −24   (d) 1

8. (a) 100   (b) 1.2   (c) 0.4

9. $N = 2h + 4c$

10. (a) $P = 3a$ (b) $Q = \frac{3a}{100}$

11. $P = 8a + 12b$

End of chapter 7 activity: Maths from stars 1 – Symmetry

The tiling patterns produced here are the basis of many Islamic designs, and form a good starting point for an investigation into these, plus some interesting cross curricular work with the Art department.

1. (a)

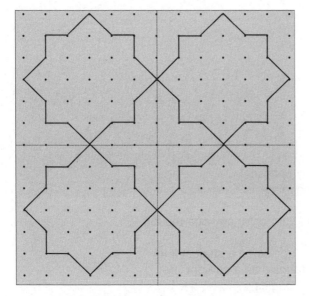

(b) Check pupils have coloured the whole design so that it still has the two lines of symmetry.

2. Check pupils' own designs.

3. (a)

(b) Check pupils have coloured the whole design so that it still has the two lines of symmetry.

4. Check pupils' own designs.
5. Check pupils' investigations of some more of the tiling patterns from the Alhambra Palace.

Chapter 8: Angles and polygons

Exercise 8.1

This type of 'angle chasing' goes down well with pupils if they are asked to 'play detective' and 'look for clues'. Calculators could be used so that the main focus is the logical thinking and is not confused with the arithmetic.

1.	$a = 126°$	$b = 91°$		
2.	$c = 62°$	$d = 46°$	$e = 62°$	
3.	$f = 71°$	$g = 109°$	$h = 71°$	
4.	$i = 128°$	$j = 52°$	$k = 76°$	
5.	$m = n = p = 60°$	$q = 120°$		
6.	$r = 48°$	$s = 110°$		
7.	$t = 60°$	$u = 38°$	$v = 38°$	$w = 104°$
8.	$x = 27°$	$y = 153°$	$z = 76.5°$	
9.	$x = 30°$			
10.	$x = 18°$	$y = 72°$	$z = 144°$	
11.	$x = 36°$	$y = 36°$	$z = 72°$	

Exercise 8.2

1.   (a) = corresponding
(c) = co-interior
(e) = alternate
(b) = none
(d) = co-interior
(f) = corresponding

2.   (a) = 110° corresponding
(c) = 120° co-interior
(e) = 125° alternate
(b) = 108° corresponding
(d) = 35° alternate
(f) = 115° co-interior

3. $a = d$, $b = c$, $e = h$, $f = g$ (all vertically opposite)
$a = e$, $c = g$, $b = f$, $d = h$ (all corresponding)
$c = f$, $d = e$ (both alternate)
There are other pairs that are equal, but not for any one reason.

4. $a + b = b + d = c + d = a + c = 180°$ (angles on a straight line)
$e + f = f + h = g + h = e + g = 180°$ (angles on a straight line)
$c + e = 180°$, $d + f = 180°$ (co-interior angles)

5. $a = d = g = 120°$ (pupils' sequence and reasons will vary)
$b = c = e = f = 60°$ (pupils' sequence and reasons will vary)

6. $a = 45°$, $h = 45°$, $b = 68°$, $e = f = 112°$, $d = g = 68°$, $c = 67°$ (order and reasons will vary)

Exercise 8.3

1. (a) Check pupils have coloured the angle ACD red.
   (b) Check pupils have coloured the angle BCA blue.
   (c) Check pupils have coloured the angle CBA yellow.

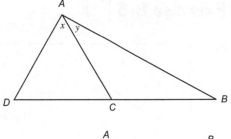

2. (a) Check pupils have coloured the angle ABD red.
   (b) Check pupils have coloured the angle CBD blue.
   (d) Check pupils have coloured the angle ADC yellow.

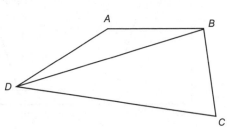

Exercise 8.4

1. (a) Angle *CDF* 72° (corresponding angles)
   (b) Angle *CDB* 108° (either co-interior or angles on a straight line)
   (c) Angle *FDE* 108° (either vertically opposite or angles on a straight line)

2. (a) Angle *ADC* 32° (alternate angles)
   (b) Angle *DCA* 74° (base angle of isosceles triangle)

3. (a) Angle *ABF* 80° (alternate angles)
   (b) Angle *CBF* 100° (co-interior angles)
   (c) Angle *CGH* 115° (co-interior angles)
   (d) Angle *CGF* 65° (various reasons)

4. (a) Angle *CED* 44° (alternate angles)
   (b) Angle *ECD* 49° (angles in a triangle)
   (c) Angle *ACB* 49° (vertically opposite)
   (d) Angle *ABC* 87° (alternate angles)

5. (a) Angle *BCA* 60° (equilateral triangle)
   (b) Angle *ACD* 60° (alternate angles)
   (c) Angle *DCE* 60° (angles on a line or corresponding angles)

6. (a) Angle *BDA* 100° (angles in a triangle)
   (b) Angle *BDC* 48° (alternate angles)
   (c) Angle *DBC* 100° (alternate angles)
   (d) Angle *BCD* 32° (angles in a triangle)

7. Angle *CED* = 61°

8. (a) Angle *GBC* 106° (co-interior angles)
   (b) Angle *CDJ* 105° (alternate angles)
   (c) Angle *BCH* 74° (co-interior angles)
   (d) Angle *CHI* 149° (alternate angles with *BCH* and *HIG*)

Exercise 8.5

1.

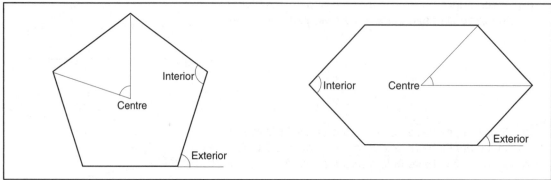

Regular pentagon   Irregular hexagon

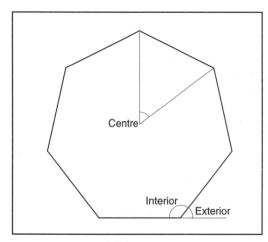

Regular heptagon

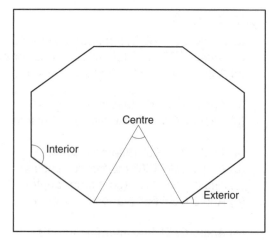

Irregular octagon

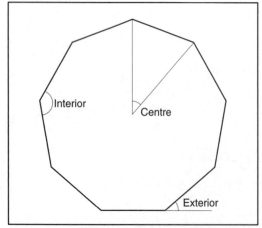

Regular nonogon

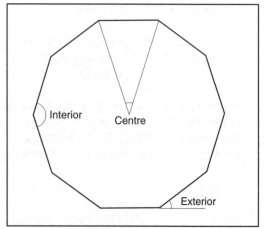

Regular decagon

2. (a) $a = 80°$ $b = 46°$ $c = 70°$ $d = 80°$ $e = 84°$

Sum = 360°

(b) $a = 54°$ $b = 55°$ $c = 74°$ $d = 65°$ $e = 69°$ $f = 43°$

Sum = 360°

(c) $a = 40°$ $b = 40°$ $c = 40°$ $d = 40°$ $e = 40°$ $f = 40°$ $g = 40°$ $h = 40°$

Sum = 360°

(d) $a = 105°$ $b = 63°$ $c = 90°$ $d = 102°$

Sum = 360°

The sum of the exterior angles of a polygon is 360°

3. (a) 72° (d) 6°
  (b) 45° (e) $51\frac{3}{7}°$
  (c) 20° (f) 18°

4. (a) 9 (d) 4
  (b) 6 (e) 18
  (c) 12 (f) 24

5. Because 65° does not go exactly into 360° and the answer must be a whole number.

6. Yes, but only if it is an equilateral triangle

Exercise 8.6

1.

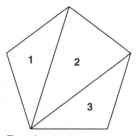

Regular pentagon

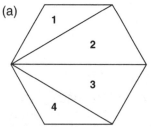

(a)

Regular hexagon
Number of sides: 6
Number of triangles: 4

(b)

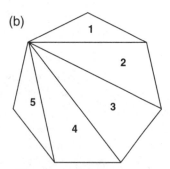

Regular heptagon
Number of sides: 7
Number of triangles: 5

(c)

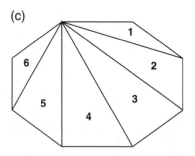

Irregular octagon
Number of sides: 8
Number of triangles: 6

(d)

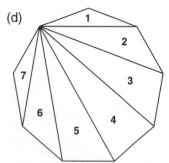

Regular nonagon
Number of sides: 9
Number of triangles: 7

(e)

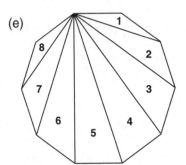

Regular decagon
Number of sides: 10
Number of triangles: 8

(f)

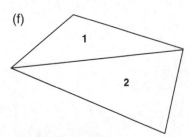

Irregular quadrilateral
Number of sides: 4
Number of triangles: 2

(g)

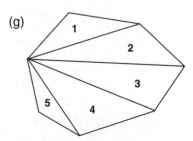

Irregular heptagon
Number of sides: 7
Number of triangles: 5

2.

Name of polygon	No. of sides of polygon	No. of triangles	Angle sum of the triangles
Pentagon	5	3	3 × 180° = 540°
(a) Hexagon	6	4	4 × 180° = 720°
(b) Heptagon	7	5	5 × 180° = 900°
(c) Octogon	8	6	6 × 180° = 1080°
(d) Nonagon	9	7	7 × 180° = 1260°
(e) Decagon	10	8	8 × 180° = 1440
(f) Quadrilateral	4	2	2 × 180° = 360°
(g) Heptagon	7	5	5 × 180° = 900°

Check the answers for any polygons the pupils may have drawn.

Angle sum of a polygon with n sides = $(n - 2) \times 180°$

3. (a) 540°   (d) 900°
     (b) 1260°   (e) 2880°
     (c) 1440°   (f) 3240

Exercise 8.7

1. (a) 120°   (d) 150°
    (b) 140°   (e) 157.5°
    (c) $128\frac{4}{7}$ °   (f) 156°
2. (a) 12   (b) 24
3. (a) 9   (b) 15   (c) 4   (d) 12
4. (a) 6   (b) 8   (c) 10   (d) 16
5. (a) 45°   (d) 36°
    (b) 72°   (e) 30°
    (c) 18°   (f) 15°

Exercise 8.8

1. (a) 72°   (b) 108°   (c) 36°   (d) 72°
2. (a) 60°   (b) 120°   (c) 30°   (d) 90°
3. (a) 60°   (b) 60°   (c) 120°   (d) 60°
4. (a) 45°   (b) 135°   (c) 45°   (d) 67.5°
5. (a) 72°   (b) 72°   (c) 108°   (d) 54°

Exercise 8.9: Maths from stars 2 – Calculating angles

Here is further investigation into the tiling patterns from the activity in Chapter 7 (page 000). The fact that angles at a point meet at 360° is very relevant here and can lead to further investigation about which regular polygons tessellate and which can meet at a point. (See Exercise 8.10)

1. 120°
2. 60°
3. 1800°
4. 240°
5. Check pupils have drawn a 6-pointed star on triangular spotty paper and that they have used it to check that their answers to Q1-4 above are correct.
6. 108°
7. $a = 72°$, $b = 36°$, $c = 36°$ and $d = 108°$
8. 135°
9. 90°, 45°, 45°
10. 2520°
11. 225°
12. 135°, 90°, 90°, 45°
13. Hexagon: 135°, 135°, 135°, 90°, 135°, 90°
    Octagon: 45°, 225°, 45°, 225°, 45°, 225°, 45°, 225°.

Exercise 8.10: Extension questions

Each of these questions can be extended as an investigation, do not expect students to do the whole thing for homework!

1. (a) Equilateral triangles and hexagons.
   (b) The interior angle of an octagon is 135° + 135° + 90° = 360°
   (c) This is an investigation into semi-regular tessellations

   You can also use a variety of regular polygons to make semi-regular tessellations. A semi-regular tessellation has two properties which are:

   1. It is formed by regular polygons.
   2. The arrangement of polygons at every vertex point is identical.

   Here are the eight semi-regular tessellations:

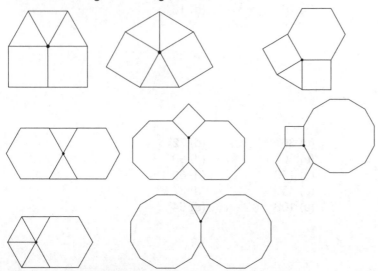

There are other combinations that seem like they should tile the plane because the arrangements of the regular polygons fill the space around a point. For example:

If you try tiling the plane with these units of tessellation you will find that they cannot be extended infinitely. To convince your students of this they should do the following with a computer graphics programme:

Step 1: Draw the polygons and save them as a group.

Step 2: Copy and paste the group.

Step 3: Rotate and position each new image so that it fits snugly into the first.

Step 4: Now continue to paste and position and see if you can tessellate it.

2.   (a) Sum of the interior angles = 720° sum of the exterior angles = 360°
         (b) 360°
         (c) 360°
         (d) You are turning the polygon inside out so that the exterior angles are now inside the shape.

3.   4, 8 and 8 and 3, 12 and 12 both work, as does 5, 5 and 10 but this one will not tile a space.

4.   (a)

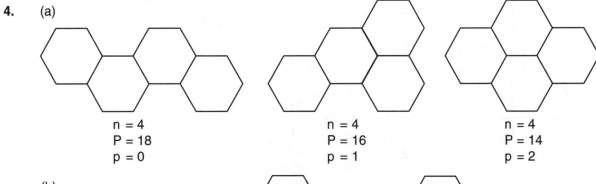

$$n = 4 \qquad\qquad n = 4 \qquad\qquad n = 4$$
$$P = 18 \qquad\qquad P = 16 \qquad\qquad P = 14$$
$$p = 0 \qquad\qquad\; p = 1 \qquad\qquad\; p = 2$$

(b)

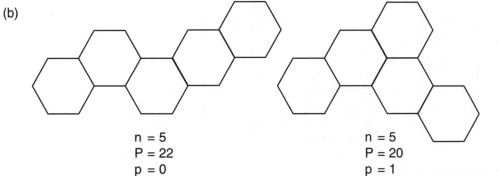

$$n = 5 \qquad\qquad\qquad n = 5$$
$$P = 22 \qquad\qquad\qquad P = 20$$
$$p = 0 \qquad\qquad\qquad\; p = 1$$

n = 5
P = 18
p = 2

n = 5
P = 16
p = 3

(c)

n = 1
P = 6
p = 0

n = 2
P = 10
p = 2

n = 3
P = 14
p = 0

n = 3
P = 12
p = 1

(d) Table of results (check pupils' drawings and answers)

n	Perimeter	p
1	0	6
2	0	10
3	0	14
3	1	12
4	0	18
4	1	16
4	2	14
5	0	22
5	1	20
5	2	18
5	3	16
6	4	18
6	3	20

(e) Perimeter = $4n - 2p + 2$

Summary Exercise 8.11

1.

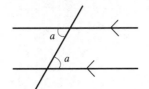

Alternative angles

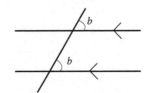

Corresponding angles

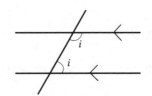

Co-interior angles

2. $a = 116°$, $b = 64°$
Check pupils' reasons why they could vary.

3. (a) 62° (b) 62° (c) 72° (d) 108°
4. (a) 40° (b) 156°
5. (a) 10° (b) 18°
6. 1980°
7. (a) 72° (b) 108° (c) 36° (d) 72°
8. (a) 54° (b) 54° (c) 72° (d) 89°
9. (a) 54° (b) 19° (c) 53.5°

End of chapter 8 activity: Nets of prisms

There is no reason why pupils should not make up nets of other prisms. This is a good activity to do close to Christmas, as you get instant mathematical decorations for your classroom.

Chapter 9: Percentages

Exercise 9.1

1. (a) 0.7, 70%   (c) 0.$\dot{6}$, 66$\frac{2}{3}$%

    (b) 0.4, 40%   (d) 0.375, 37.5%

2. (a) 27%, $\frac{27}{100}$ (c) 65%, $\frac{13}{20}$

    (b) 70%, $\frac{7}{10}$ (d) 60%, $\frac{3}{5}$

3. (a) 0.4, $\frac{2}{5}$ (c) 0.84, $\frac{21}{25}$

    (b) 0.55, $\frac{11}{20}$ (d) 0.24, $\frac{6}{25}$

4. (a) 0.16, 16%   (c) 0.925, 92.5%

    (b) 0.45, 45%   (d) 1.2, 120%

5. (a) 119%, 1$\frac{19}{100}$ (c) 260%   2$\frac{3}{5}$

    (b) 32.5% $\frac{13}{40}$ (d) 77% $\frac{77}{100}$

6. (a) 0.43, $\frac{43}{100}$ (c) 0.375, $\frac{3}{8}$

    (b) 0., $\frac{2}{3}$ (d) 1.125, 1$\frac{1}{8}$

Exercise 9.2

There are other ways to calculate percentages, such as finding 10% and then 5%, and you may wish to revise these. However the main purpose of this chapter is to use calculator methods.

1. 20 cm   6.   £3.20
2. £80   7.   1.4 kg
3. 175 g   8.   2.8 km
4. £600   9.   £255
5. 3.2 m   10. 2.4 m

Exercise 9.3

1.	67.5 cm	**6.**	£5.07
2.	£3.96	**7.**	7.688 kg
3.	17.5 g	**8.**	0.3045 km or 304.5 m
4.	£94.50	**9.**	£288.36
5.	2.05 m	**10.**	1.05 m

Exercise 9.4

Do emphasise the importance of reading and answering the question.

1. 144 boys, 156 girls
2. 24p
3. £4 cheaper (so new price is £16)
4. 52
5. 12
6. £5.76
7. 144
8. 70
9. 144 000
10. 36 000

Exercise 9.5

1. 40%
2. 12.5%
3. 25%
4. 12.5%
5. 66%
6. 62.5%
7. 20%
8. 69.2%
9. 12.5%
10. 25.0%
11. 7%
12. 78.3%
13. 78.9%
14. 27.3%
15. 75%
16. 8
17. Very accurate
18. You cannot tell because it depends who you asked.

Exercise 9.6

1. (a) 25%   (b) 60%   (c) 100%   (d) 60%
2. (a) 40%   (b) 32%   (c) 25%   (d) 25%
3. (a) £11.75   (b) £9.60   (c) £30   (d) £23
4. 16%, $\frac{2}{3}$ the same
5. £10.50
6. 20%
7. 60%
8. (a) £10   (b) £135
9. £14.70
10. £30
11. (a) £7200   (b) £6336   (c) 29.6%
12. (a) £200   (b) £160   (c) 8% (you effectively have £360 less than you might have had)
13. 82p
14. 156%
15. (a) 30p   (b) £2
16. £2.96

Exercise 9.7: Extension questions

1. 15 g
2. £75
3. 22 m
4. 96 litres
5. 210 grams

6. £5
7. £5
8. 0.25 km
9. 4 g
10. 0.5 litres

11. £2.10
12. 73.125 m
13. 1.26 kg
14. £731.40
15. 1.53925 km

16. £6.13
17. £4.39
18. 15.925 tonnes
19. 7.83 kg
20. 0.9625 litres

Exercise 9.8: Summary exercise

Pupils should NOT use a calculator for questions 1 to 6

1. (a) $\frac{7}{20}$ (c) $\frac{21}{50}$

    (b) $\frac{3}{25}$ (d) $\frac{1}{8}$

2. (a) 0.82   (c) 0.875
    (b) 0.375   (d) 0.28

3. (a) 150%   (c) $33\frac{1}{3}$%
    (b) 12.5%   (d) 24%

4. (a) £3.50   (d) 225 km
    (b) 70 g   (e) £50
    (c) 960 people (f) 300 miles

5. 12
6. 70%
7. 15
8. 40%
9. £18.20
10. 42.9%
11. (a) 70 cm   (b) 84 cm   (c) 1.68 m
12. 66% loss

End of chapter 9 activity: Tormenting tessellations

This is fun to do on a computer, as well as by drawing. There are a lot of web sites on tessellations which could provide some inspiration.

Chapter 10: Ratio and enlargement

Exercise 10.1

1.	(a) 1:5	(b) 5:1	(c) 500 ml	(d) 600 ml	(e) 200 ml	(f) 3.75 l
2.	(a) 1:3	(b) 3:1	(c) 300 ml	(d) 400 ml	(e) 333 ml	(f) 2.25 l
3.	(a) 1:20	(b) 20:1	(c) 2 litres	(d) 50 ml	(e) 8 l	

Exercise 10.2

1. (a) 4 : 1   (b) 1 : 4   (c) 1 : 2   (d) 2 : 1
2. (a) 4 : 3   (b) 3 :4   (c) 3 : 2   (d) 2 : 3
3. (a) 3 : 2   (b) 2 : 3   (c) 5 : 2   (d) 2 : 5
4. (a) 3 : 5   (b) 5 : 2   (c) 10 : 7   (d) 2 : 11
5. (a) 6 : 7   (b) 4 : 3   (c) 11 : 9
6. (a) 7 : 12   (b) 7 : 25   (c) 7 : 3
7. (a) 2 : 3 = 40 : 60   (b) 2 : 7 = 14 : 49   (c) 5 : 8 = 25 : 40
8. (a) 22: 33 = 2 : 3   (b) 21: 7 = 3 : 1   (c) 25 : 80 = 5 : 16
9. There may be more than one correct answer:
    (a) 2 : 3 = 14 : 21   (b) 15 : 40 = 3 : 8   (c) 35 : 70 = 5 : 10
       or   or   or
       3 : 2 = 21 : 14   15 : 25 = 3 : 5   35 : 50 = 7 : 1

Exercise 10.3

1. 4 : 3
2. (a) 1: 4   (b) 1 : 1   (c) 1 : 9
3. 2 : 3
4. 5 : 4
5. (a) 1 : 4   (b) 1 : 5

6. (a) 1 : 1   (b) 1 : 2
7. 5 : 8
8. 10 : 7
9. (a) 3 : 1   (b) 1 : 3
10. (a) 1 : 7   (b) 1 : 8

Exercise 10.4

1. (a) $\frac{14}{8} = \frac{7}{4}$ (b) $\frac{16}{23} = \frac{4}{3}$ (c) $\frac{15}{45} = \frac{3}{9}$

2. (a) $\frac{14}{56} = \frac{1}{4}$ (b) $\frac{16}{72} = \frac{2}{9}$ (c) $\frac{80}{144} = \frac{5}{9}$

3. (a) $\frac{3}{2}$ (b) $\frac{2}{3}$ (c) $\frac{2}{5}$ (d) $\frac{3}{2} \times \frac{3}{5}$

4. (a) 3 : 4   (b) $\frac{2}{9}$ (c) 1 : 2   (d) 4 : 3 : 2

   (e) You cannot have 3 levels

Exercise 10.5

1.
   A B C

2.
   A B C

3.
   A B C

4.
   A B C

5.
   A B C

6.
   A B C

7. (a) 1 : 2   (b) 2 : 1   (c) 1 : 3   (d) 2 : 3

8. (a) 1 : 3   (b) 3 : 1   (c) 1 : 4   (d) 3 : 4

9. AC = 14 cm and BC = 10 cm

10. (a) 8 cm (b) 14 cm

Exercise 10.6

1. Elder £65 and younger £35
2. 20 kg 120 kg
3. 5 : 8
4. 1.5 l
5. 80 ml
6. (a) 125 ml   (b) 175 ml   (c) 70 ml
7. 135 cm²

8. 21 litres of blue, 27 litres of green
9. 8 litres Lily White and 20 litres Buttercup
10. 450 mg
11. 30°, 60°, 90° right-angled triangle
12. 36°, 72°, 72° isosceles triangle.

Exercise 10.7

1. 1 : 100 000
2. 1 : 100
3. 1 : 50 000
4. 1 : 5
5. 1 : 500
6. 1 : 500 000
7. 1 : 50

Exercise 10.8

1. (a) 12 m   (b) 20 cm   (c) 15 m   (d) 1 cm   (e) 4
2. (a) 50 cm   (b) 4 cm   (c) 60 cm   (d) 5 m by 7 m   (e) 2
3. 4.4 mm
4. 3.5 mm
5. (a) 100 m   (b) 40 cm   (c) 320 m   (d) 24 cm   (e) 2
6. 1 cm to 50 m
7. (a) 20 cm   (b) 5 cm   (c) 30 cm and 37.5 cm tall.   (d) 2
8. (a) 2 feet   (b) 10 inches   (c) 9 feet   (d) 7.5 inches

Exercise 10.9

1. 126 miles
2. 60p
3. 210 bricks
4. 27 tins
5. It depends how fast they run.
6. 75 min
7. 2.1 m, if it grows at the same rate, but it probably will not.
8. 274.5 miles
9. 75 minutes
10. It depends how much time I spend reading and the length of the books. (Perhaps about $5\frac{1}{2}$ books.)
11. About 15.4 gallons
12. 8 tins of soup
13. 336 lb
14. 5 men
15. 375 g of self raising flour

    375 ml water

    6 tablespoons of milk

    2 eggs ($1\frac{1}{2}$)

Exercise 10.10

1. Pupils should have drawn a line 6 cm long.

2. Pupils should have drawn a line 4 cm long.

3. Pupils should have drawn a line 6 cm long.

4. (a)   (b)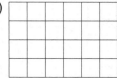

5.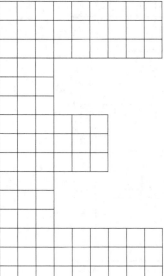

6.

7. (a) 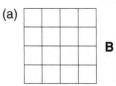   (b) 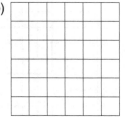   (c)

8. A: 4; B: 16; C: 36; D: 9
   (a) 1 : 4   (b) 1 : 9   (c) 4 : 9
   The area scale factor is the square of the linear scale factor.

Exercise 10.11: Enlargement on a grid

1.

(a)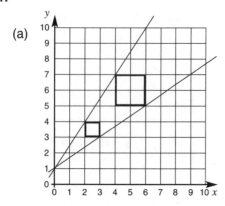

Centre of enlargement (0, 1)

Scale factor 2

(b)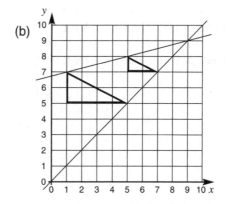

Centre of enlargement (9, 9)

Scale factor 2

(c)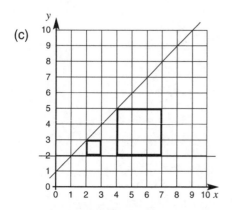

Centre of enlargement (1, 2)

Scale factor 3

(d)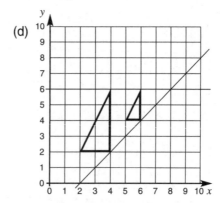

Centre of enlargement (8, 6)

Scale factor 2

(e)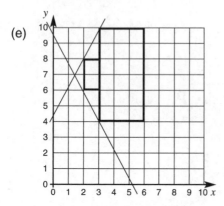

Centre of enlargement $(1\frac{1}{2}, 7)$

Scale factor 3

(f)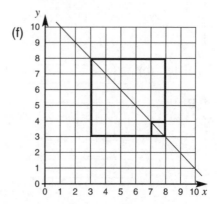

Centre of enlargement (8, 3)

Scale factor 5

2. (a)

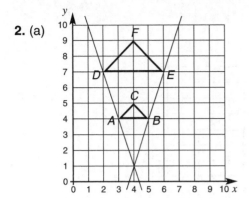

   (b)   Centre of enlargement (4, 1)

           Scale factor 2

5. (a)

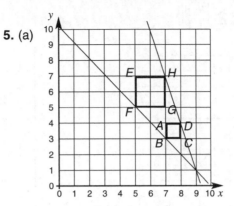

   (b)   Centre of enlargement (9, 1)

           Scale factor 2

3. (a)

   (b)   Centre of enlargement (2, 3)

           Scale factor 3

6. (a)

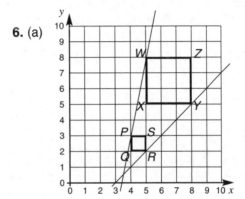

   (b)   Centre of enlargement $(3\frac{1}{2}, \frac{1}{2})$

           Scale factor 3

4. (a)

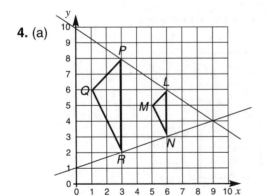

   (b)   Centre of enlargement (9, 4)

           Scale factor 2

7. (a)

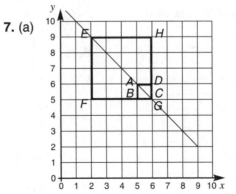

   (b)   Centre of enlargement (6, 5)

           Scale factor 4

Exercise 10.12

1. (a)

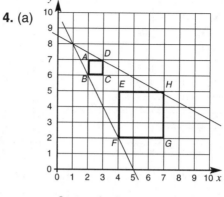

Centre of enlargement (0, 0)
Scale factor 3

(b) Ratio of area EFG : area ABC 9 : 1.

4. (a)

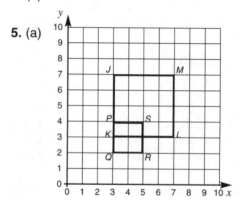

Centre of enlargement (1, 8)
Scale factor 2

(b) Ratio of area EFGH : area ABCD 9 : 1

2. (a)

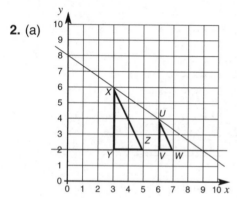

Centre of enlargement (9, 2)
Scale factor 2

(b) Ratio of area XYZ : area UVW 4 : 1

5. (a)

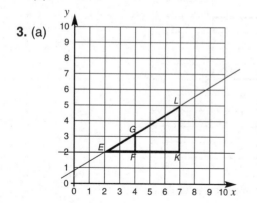

Centre of enlargement (3, 1)
Scale factor 2

(b) Ratio of area JKLM : area PQRS 4 : 1

3. (a)

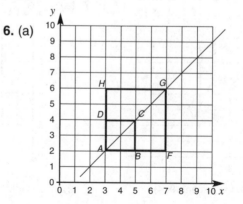

Centre of enlargement (2, 2)
Scale factor 3

(b) Ratio of area EKL : area EFG 9 : 1

6. (a)

Centre of enlargement (3, 2)
Scale factor 2

(b) Ratio of area AFGH : area ABCD 4 : 1

7. The ratio of the areas is the square of the ratio of the sides.

Exercise 10.13: Extension questions 1

1. 51 kg copper, 136 kg zinc
2. 3 jugs (or 2.25 jugs if you accept parts)
3. 555 (556 to 3 sig. figs.)
4. 36°, 72°, 108°, 144°.
5. 60°. 90°, 90° 120°.
   It is a right-angled trapezium. It could be a kite if the order of the angles does not matter.
6. Colonel Mustard 80 ml, Mrs Mustard 33 ml

Exercise 10.14: Extension questions 2 – Ratio and algebra

1. (a) 27   (b) 41   (c) 162

2. (a) 49   (b) 27   (c) 105

3. (a) $3x$ (b) $3y$ (c) $x: y$ (d) $x: y$
   (e) 1 : 3   (f) 1 : 3   (g) yes

4. $x = 19.2$ and $y = 1.6$

5. $x = 4.5$ $y = 6.75$ and $z = 1.5$
   1 : 2.25

6. (a) The scale factor is 2.5   (b) $v = 2$, $y = 5$ and $z = 8.75$

Exercise 10.15: Summary exercise

1. (a) 4 : 7   (b) 7 : 4   (c) 7 : 11
2. (a) 1 : 2   (b) 2 : 9   (c) 12 : 5
3. 2 km
4.

```
L_____I_____I
A        B                C
```

5.

```
L_____I_____I
A                        B                                      C
```

6. Replace the in these ratios:
   (a) 34: 17 = 2:1   (b) 24 : 8 = 6 : 2   (c) 2 : 7 = 34 : 119

7. 45 cm and 75 cm

8. 19.2 l

9. 3.45 cm if the rain falls at the same rate

10.

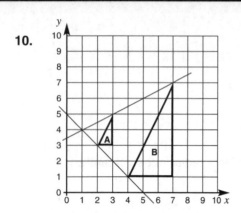

End of chapter 10 activity: Christmas lunch investigation

House number	Arrangements
1	1
2	1
3	1
4	3
5	12
6	60
7	360

The pupils should check their pattern is correct by drawing all the arrangements for the family of seven. As they start to do this it will become apparent quite quickly that it will take for ages. Let the pupils go over their previous results and see the pattern:

House number	Arrangements
1	1
2	2 choices for A, 1 choice for B. $2 \times 1 = 2$; halved, since clockwise and anti-clockwise are the same, $\rightarrow 1$
3	3 choices for A, 2 choices for B, 1 choice for C. $3 \times 2 \times 1 = 6$; halved $\rightarrow 3$, then divided by 3 $\rightarrow 1$
4	4 choices for A, 3 choices for B, 2 choices for C, 1 choice for D. $4 \times 3 \times 2 \times 1$; halved $\rightarrow 12$, then divided by 4 $\rightarrow 3$
5	5 choices for A ... $5 \times 4 \times 3 \times 2 \times 1 = 120$; halved $\rightarrow 60$, then divided by 5 $\rightarrow 12$
6	6 choices for A ... $6 \times 5 \times 4 \times 3 \times 2 \times 1 = 720$; halved $\rightarrow 360$, then divided by 6 $\rightarrow 60$
7	7 choices for A ... $7 \times 6 \times 5 \times 4 \times 3 \times 2 \times 1 = 5040$; halved $\rightarrow 2520$, then divided by 7 $\rightarrow 360$

It might be worth introducing potential scholars to the factorial button of their calculator as these questions often arise on papers.

Chapter 11: Algebra 2 – Equations and brackets

Exercise 11.1

1. $3x = 3$
2. $2x + 6$
3. $2x - 6$
4. $12 + 4x$
5. $10 - 2a$

6. $6b + 3$
7. $8x + 6$
8. $10 + 4a$
9. $10y + 15$
10. $21 - 9a$

11. $24 + 12a$
12. $4x - 6y$
13. $12a - 3b$
14. $10x + 5$
15. $3b - 15a$

16. $21 - 6x$
17. $12a - 6b$
18. $24 - 18x$
19. $16n - 32m$
20. $15p - 5q$

Exercise 11.2

1. $3x + 8$
2. $6x - 2$
3. $7x - 15$
4. $5x + 10$
5. $3x + 3$

6. $12 - 3x$
7. $14 - 6x$
8. -16
9. $8x$
10. $18x + 10$

11. $14x - 6$
12. $7x + 8$
13. $27 - 2x$
14. $7x + 8$
15. $11x + 15$

16. $5x + 21$
17. $20x + 16$
18. $28 - 24x$
19. $7x + 31$
20. $15 - 4x$

Exercise 11.3

1. $2 - 2x$
2. $x - 4$
3. $x - 10$
4. $2 - 9x$
5. $2 - 2x$

6. $3x - 4$
7. $x - 6$
8. $-12x$
9. $10 - x$
10. $2 - 7x$

11. $5x + 9$
12. $4 - x$
13. $14x - 4$
14. $3x - 1$
15. $3x + 3$

16. $18 - 7x$
17. 5
18. $4x$
19. 10
20. 0

Exercise 11.4

1. $6x - 4$
2. $8 - 4x$
3. $7x - 1$
4. $5x + 8$
5. $4x + 8$

6. $16 - 2x$
7. $7x + 10$
8. 7
9. $11x$
10. $11 - 3x$

11. $8x$
12. -2
13. $48x - 3$
14. $6x$
15. $-10x - 15$

16. $14x$
17. $3x - 6$
18. $24x - 8$
19. $9x$
20. 0

Exercise 11.5

1.   (a) $2x + 6 = 2(x + \mathbf{3})$ (d) $3x + 6 = 3(x + \mathbf{2})$

     (b) $3x + 12 = 3(x + \mathbf{4})$ (e) $6x + 8 = 2(\mathbf{3}x + 4)$

     (c) $4x - 8 = 4(\mathbf{x} - 2)$ (f) $14 - 8x = 2(\mathbf{7} - 4x)$

2.   (a) $3x + 12 = \mathbf{3}(x + 4)$ (d) $15 - 3x = \mathbf{3}(5 - y)$

     (b) $6x - 3 = \mathbf{3}(2x - 1)$ (e) $8x + 2 = \mathbf{2}(4x + 1)$

     (c) $4x + 2y - 6 = \mathbf{2}(2x + y - 3)$

3.   (a) $4x + 6 = 2(\mathbf{2}x + 3)$ (d) $12 + x = 3(\mathbf{4} + 3x)$

     (b) $3x - 15 = 3(x - \mathbf{5})$ (e) $24 + 16x = 8(\mathbf{3} + 2x)$

     (c) $6x + 9y - 12 = 3(\mathbf{2}x + \mathbf{3}y - \mathbf{4})$

4.   (a) $3x + xy = \mathbf{x}(3 + y)$ (c) $15p - 7pq = \mathbf{p}(15 - 7q)$

     (b) $ab - 7a = \mathbf{a}(b - 7)$ (d) $3abc - 4b = \mathbf{b}(3ac - 4)$

5.   (a) $2x + xy = x(2 + y)$ (d) $pq + 6q = q(\mathbf{p} + \mathbf{6})$

     (b) $ab + 12a = 1(b + \mathbf{12})$ (e) $5y - 3xy = y(\mathbf{5} - \mathbf{3}x)$

     (c) $5ab + a = 1(\mathbf{5}b + 1)$ (f) $4ab - a = a(\mathbf{4}b - \mathbf{1})$

6.   (a) $3x + 6xy = \mathbf{3}x(1 + 2y)$ (c) $15p - 3pq = \mathbf{3}p(5 - q)$

     (b) $21ab - 7a = \mathbf{7}a(3b - 1)$ (d) $3abc - 12b = \mathbf{3}b(ac - 4)$

7.   (a) $2x + 6xy = 2x(1 + \mathbf{3y})$ (c) $12pq + 6q = 3q(\mathbf{4p + 2})$

      (b) $3ab + 12a = 3a(\mathbf{b + 4})$ (d) $15y - 25xy = 5y(\mathbf{3 - 5x})$

8.   (a) $4(x + 2)$ (b) $3(y - 2)$ (c) $6(2 + 3y)$

9.   (a) $x(4 + y)$ (b) $a(3b - 7)$ (c) $x(3 + 14y + z)$

10.   (a) $2x(4 + y)$ (b) $4a(3b - 2)$ (c) $3x(1+ 3y + 2z)$

11.   (a) $5(3y + 1)$ (d) $4 x(4 - 5y)$

      (b) $8a(3 - 2b)$ (e) $2a(4 + 2b - 3c)$

      (c) $4(4x - 5xy + 1)$ (f) $4(2x + y - 3xy)$

12.   (a) $2(x + 4)$ (g) $8(a + 2b - 3ab)$

      (b) $x (17 + 14y)$ (h) $6ab(3c + 1)$

      (c) Not possible   (i) $a(9a + 16)$

      (d) $3(5 - 7x)$ (j) $2a(9a + 8b)$

      (e) Not possible   (k) $4x(x + 4y)$

      (f) $2a(9 + 8b)$ (l) $8p(q + 2p)$

      (m) $4a(4b - 1)$ (s) Not possible

      (n) $3a(8 - 5b)$ (t) $3p(4q - 1 + 3s)$

      (o) $6(3 + 2a)$ (u) $3x(5 + 3y^2)$

      (p) $y(14x + 15)$ (v) Not possible

      (g) $3(5x + 8 - 3y)$ (w) $3x(8x - 3y + 6)$

      (r) Not possible   (x) $5a(3a - b^2 + 2b)$

Exercise 11.6

1.   2   6.   3

2.   9   7.   11

3.   2   8.   4

4.   5   9.   −1

5.   −4   10.   1

11. 2   16.   3

12.	2	17.	7
13.	2	18.	2
14.	−2	19.	1
15.	$-2\frac{1}{2}$	20.	2

21.	1	26.	−1
22.	$1\frac{1}{3}$	27.	$\frac{1}{2}$
23.	−3	28.	4
24.	$1\frac{1}{4}$	29.	−1
25.	$-1\frac{1}{2}$	30.	−1

Exercise 11.7

1.	±4	6.	±0.5
2.	±5	7.	±12
3.	±100	8.	10 000
4.	0.16	9.	0.01
5.	1.44	10.	±11

11.	$\frac{1}{4}$	14.	$\pm\frac{1}{5}$
12.	$\pm\frac{1}{3}$	15.	± 0.06
13.	$\frac{1}{100}$	16.	$\frac{4}{9}$

Exercise 11.8: Solving equations with x^2

1.	$x = 1$ or -1	6.	$a = 8$ or -8
2.	$a = 10$ or -10	7.	$x = 0.3$ or -0.3
3.	$b = 7$ or -7	8.	$c = 40$ or -40
4.	$c = 9$ or -9	9.	$b = 0.4$ or -0.4
5.	$y = 2$ or -2	10.	$y = 20$ or -20

11.	12 m
12.	1.2 m
13.	0.8 cm
14.	0.8 cm

Exercise 11.9

1.	3		4.	3
2.	8		5.	5
3.	1		6.	1

7. $\frac{1}{2}$ 10. $-2\frac{1}{8}$

8. $3\frac{1}{2}$ 11. $5\frac{1}{5}$

9. $\frac{2}{3}$ 12. $-1\frac{1}{2}$

13. $-1\frac{1}{2}$ 16. $-\frac{1}{6}$

14. 2   17. $-1\frac{1}{2}$

15. $-\frac{1}{3}$ 18. $\frac{1}{3}$

19. 5   23. $-\frac{2}{3}$

20. 1   24. 3

21. −1   25. $1\frac{5}{6}$

22. $-\frac{1}{3}$ 26. 1

Exercise 11.10

1.	10		6.	9
2.	14		7.	$1\frac{1}{3}$
3.	27		8.	1
4.	20		9.	19
5.	6		10.	3

Exercise 11.11

1. $1\frac{2}{3}$ 6. $-1\frac{1}{3}$

2. $1\frac{3}{4}$ 7. $-4\frac{1}{4}$

3. 3   8. $-1\frac{1}{6}$

4. 0   9. 2

5. $-5\frac{1}{2}$ 10. −3

11.	3	**16.**	$3\frac{3}{4}$
12.	$-8\frac{2}{5}$	**17.**	-3
13.	1	**18.**	11
14.	$-\frac{13}{18}$	**19.**	$1\frac{4}{7}$
15.	3	**20.**	-1

Exercise 11.12

1. $2(x + 5) = 30$ $\qquad$ $x = 10$, so my number was 10

2. $2x + 5 = 25$ $\qquad$ $x = 10$, so my number was 10

3. $2(x - 3) = 14$ $\qquad$ $x = 10$, so my number was 10

4. $2x - 3 = 17$ $\qquad$ $x = 10$, so my number was 10

5. $2(x + 4) = 40$ $\qquad$ $x = 16$, so I am 16

6. $3(x - 4) = 36$ $\qquad$ $x = 16$, so I am 16

7. (a) $x - 5$

(b) $2(x - 5)$

(c) $4x - 15$

(d) $4x - 15 = 33$ $\qquad$ $x = 12$, so my sister is 12

(e) I am 7, my brother is 14

8. (a) $x - 3$ $\qquad\qquad$ (b) $3(x - 3)$ $\qquad\qquad$ (c) $5x - 12$

(d) $5x - 12 = 28$ $\qquad\quad$ (e) 15
$\quad\;\; x = 8$, so I am 8

9. (a) $2x$ $\qquad\qquad\qquad$ (b) $2x - 5$ $\qquad\qquad$ (c) $5x - 5$

(d) $5x - 5 = 15$
$\quad$ Tom had 4, I had 8 and Sally had 3 sweets

Exercise 11.13: Extension questions – Working with fractions

1.	5	**6.**	7
2.	$4\frac{5}{6}$	**7.**	$5\frac{1}{2}$
3.	3	**8.**	13
4.	$5\frac{1}{3}$	**9.**	$\frac{2}{3}$
5.	–2	**10.**	$3\frac{5}{6}$

Exercise 11.14: Summary exercise

1.   (a) $2x + 2$ (b) $6x - 12$ (c) $20 + 12x$

2.   (a) $5x + 2$ (c) $-6x - 5$
       (b) $4x + 1$ (d) $24 - 2x$

3.   (a) $2(a + 2)$ (e) $3(8a + 5b - 7c)$
       (b) $3(b - 6c)$ (f) $5x(2y - x)$
       (c) $z(4 + y)$ (g) Not possible
       (d) Not possible   (h) $8a(1 + 2b - 3a)$

4.   (a) 4   (c) 17
       (b) 3   (d) $\frac{3}{4}$

5.   (a) 4   (c) –4
       (b) 2   (d) $\frac{1}{5}$

6.   (a) 20   (b) $3\frac{1}{2}$

7.   Solve these equations:
       (a) $-\frac{1}{2}$ (b) –1   (c) 1

8. $2x + 7 = 15$ $x = 4$, so my number was 4

9.   (a) $x + 6$ (b) $x - 10$ (c) $3x - 4$
       (d) $3x - 4 = 41$
             $3x = 45$
              $x = 15$
   Therefore Henry walked 15 miles, Casper 5 miles and Freddy 21 miles.

End of chapter 11 activity: Dungeons and dragons

This is an interesting investigation in that it generates a simple formula, but with some limits.

1.

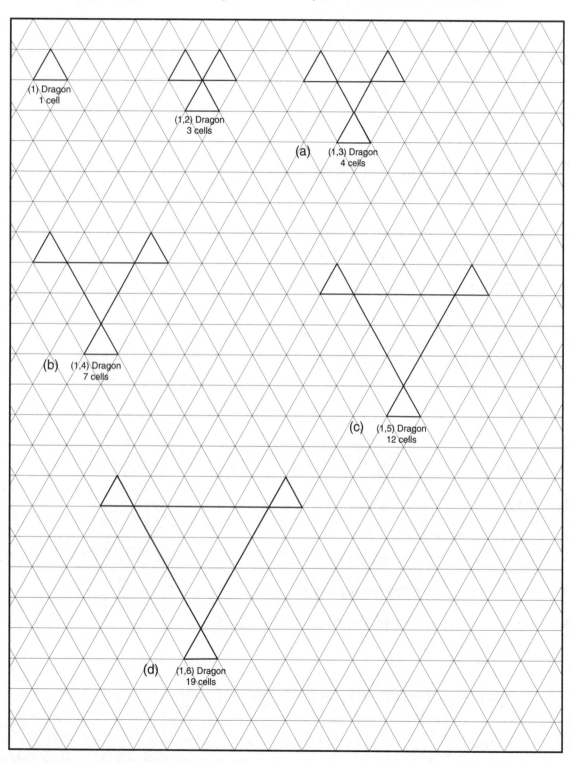

(1) Dragon
1 cell

(1,2) Dragon
3 cells

(a) (1,3) Dragon
4 cells

(b) (1,4) Dragon
7 cells

(c) (1,5) Dragon
12 cells

(d) (1,6) Dragon
19 cells

2. and 3. Learner dragon table:

Dragon	Units walked in one circuit	Dungeons guarded
(1,1)	3	1
(1,2)	9	3
(1,3)	12	4
(1,4)	15	7
(1,5)	18	12
(1,6)	21	19
(1,7)	24	28

4.

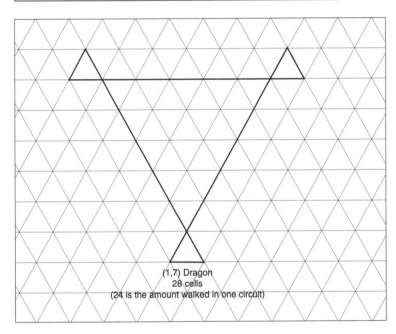

(1,7) Dragon
28 cells
(24 is the amount walked in one circuit)

5. A (1,10) dragon will guard 67 dungeons

6. $(n - 2)^2 + 3$ when n >1

7.

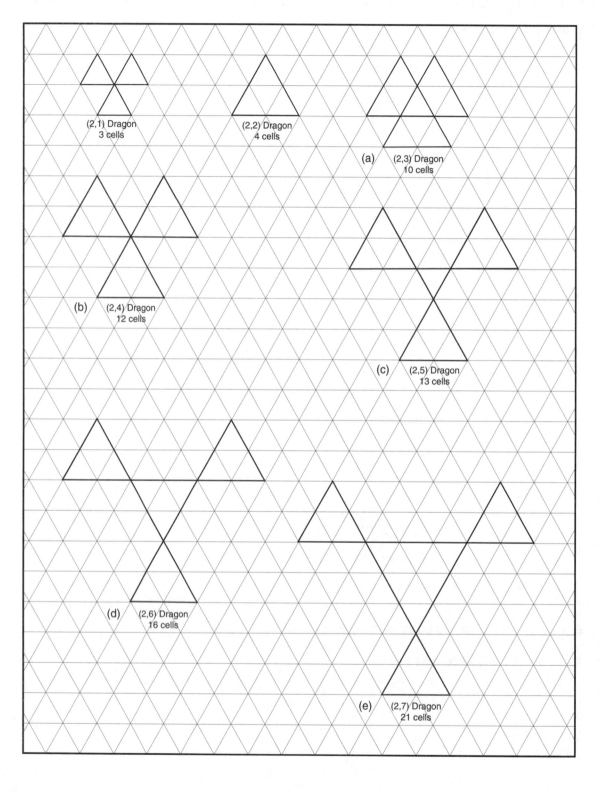

(2,1) Dragon
3 cells

(2,2) Dragon
4 cells

(a) (2,3) Dragon
10 cells

(b) (2,4) Dragon
12 cells

(c) (2,5) Dragon
13 cells

(d) (2,6) Dragon
16 cells

(e) (2,7) Dragon
21 cells

Dragon	Distance walked in one circuit (units)	Dungeons guarded
(2 , 1)	9	3
(2 , 2)	6	4
(2 , 3)	15	10
(2 , 4)	18	12
(2 , 5)	21	13
(2 , 6)	24	16
(2 , 7)	27	21

8. A (2,10) dragon will walk 36 units and guard 48 dungeons.

   Formula for a megadragon:

   $(n - 4)^2 + 12$ when $n > 3$

9. $(n - 2m)^2 + 3m$ when $n > 2m - 1$

Chapter 12: Scale drawing and bearings

Exercise 12.1: How to use a compass 1
Practical

Exercise 12.2: How to use a compass 2
Practical

Exercise 12.3: How to use a compass 3
Practical

Exercise 12.4: Using bearings

Warning: These answers depend on the worksheets having been printed at 100% (i.e. not enlarged or reduced to fit paper size). See instructions on the Worksheet CD.

Object	Bearing	Distance	
		Measured	Actual
Boat	063°	5.4 cm	0.54 km
Tanker	135°	4.8 cm	0.48 km
Lighthouse	224°	5 cm	0.5 km
Hilltop	305°	3.7 cm	0.37 km

Exercise 12.5

1.

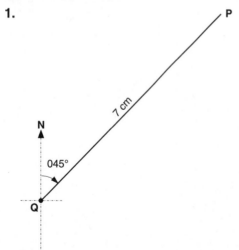

2.

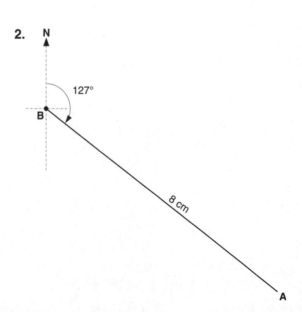

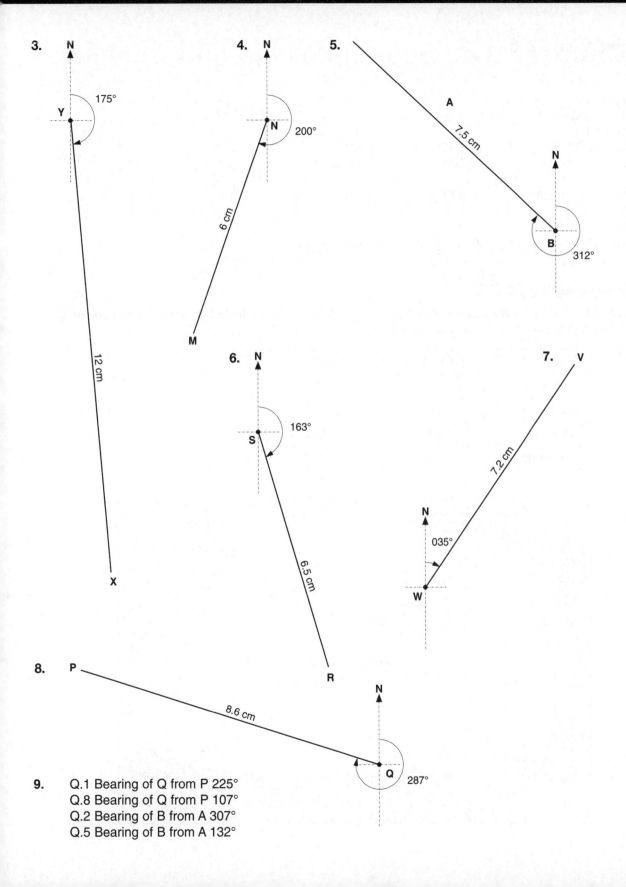

3.

175°

Y

12 cm

X

4.

N

200°

6 cm

M

5.

A

7.5 cm

N

B 312°

6.

N

S 163°

6.5 cm

R

7.

V

7.2 cm

N

035°

W

8.

P

8.6 cm

N

Q 287°

9.   Q.1 Bearing of Q from P 225°
         Q.8 Bearing of Q from P 107°
         Q.2 Bearing of B from A 307°
         Q.5 Bearing of B from A 132°

Exercise 12.6

1. 300°
2. 252°
3. 033°
4. 118°
5. (a) 172°   (b) 289°   (c) 109°
6. (a) (i) 290°   (ii) 020°   (iii) 110°
   (b) 065°
7. (a) (i) 228°   (ii) 342°   (b) 105°
8. 037°
9. 90° clockwise
10. 097°. 6 km. You have walked an equilateral triangle.

Exercise 12.7

Warning: These answers depend on the worksheets having been printed at 100% (i.e. not enlarged or reduced to fit paper size). See instructions on the Worksheet CD.

1.

Object	Bearing of object	Bearing from object
Boathouse	058°	238°
Rescue station	118°	298°
Jetty	232°	052°
Telephone	318°	138°

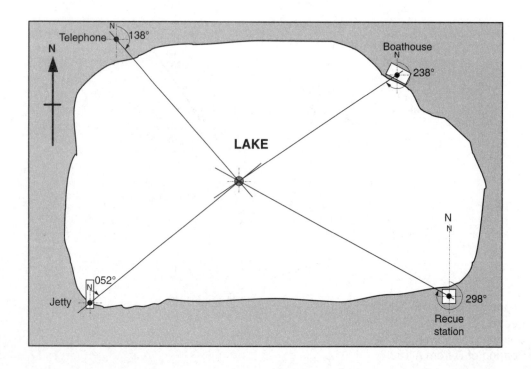

Object	Distance	
	Measured	Actual
Boathouse	5.9 cm	118 m
Rescue station	7 cm	140 m
Jetty	4.7 cm	94 m
Telephone	5.3 cm	106 m

2.

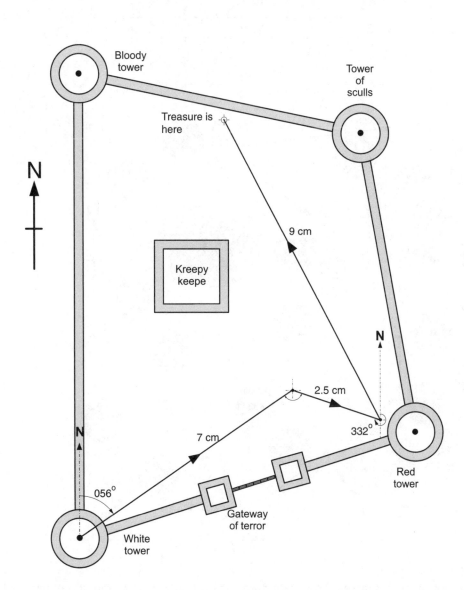

3.

Leg No:	bearing	distance	
		actual	to scale
1	097°	40 m	8 cm
2	234°	30 m	6 cm
3	180°	15 m	3 cm
4	127°	27.5 m	5.5 cm
5	075°	15 m	3 cm
6	134°	15 m	3 cm

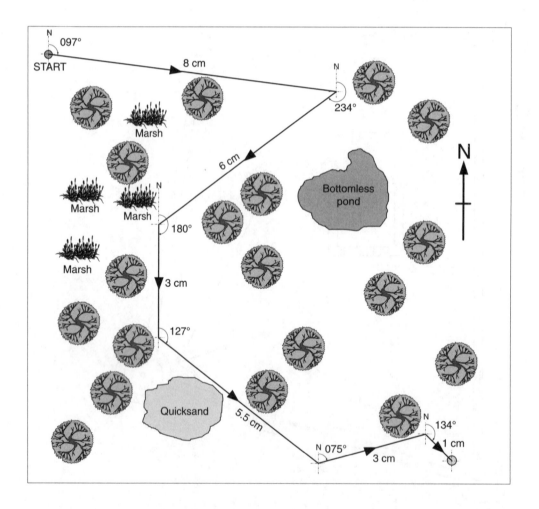

4.   Check pupils' drawings and tables. There are many possible alternatives that the pupils could give as ways of getting back to the start without crossing the original line.

Exercise 12.8

1.

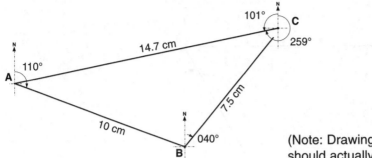

(Note: Drawing shown is half the size pupils should actually have drawn.)

2. (a)-(c)

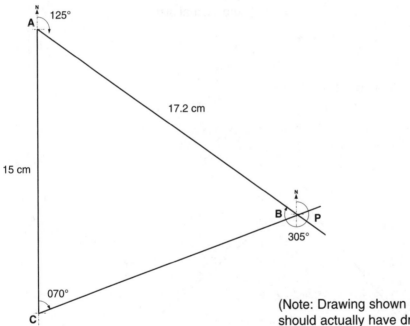

(Note: Drawing shown is half the size pupils should actually have drawn.)

(d) Distance from A to P is 17.2 km and the bearing from A is 125°.

3. (a)-(c)

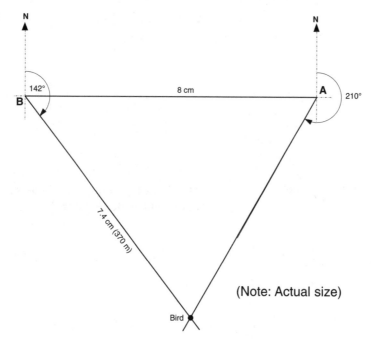

(Note: Actual size)

(d) Distance from the bird to point B is 370 m.

4. (a)-(c)

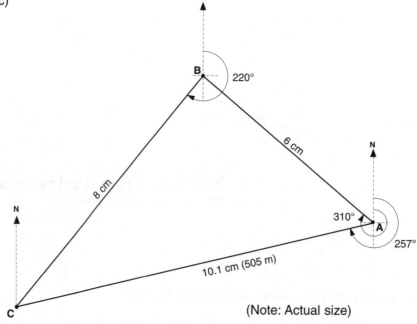

(Note: Actual size)

(d) 505 m

(e) Bearing of C from A is 257°.

5.

Length of second leg is 7.8 km on a bearing of 198° from Y.

(Note: Drawing shown is half the size pupils should actually have drawn.)

6.   127°

(Note: Actual size)

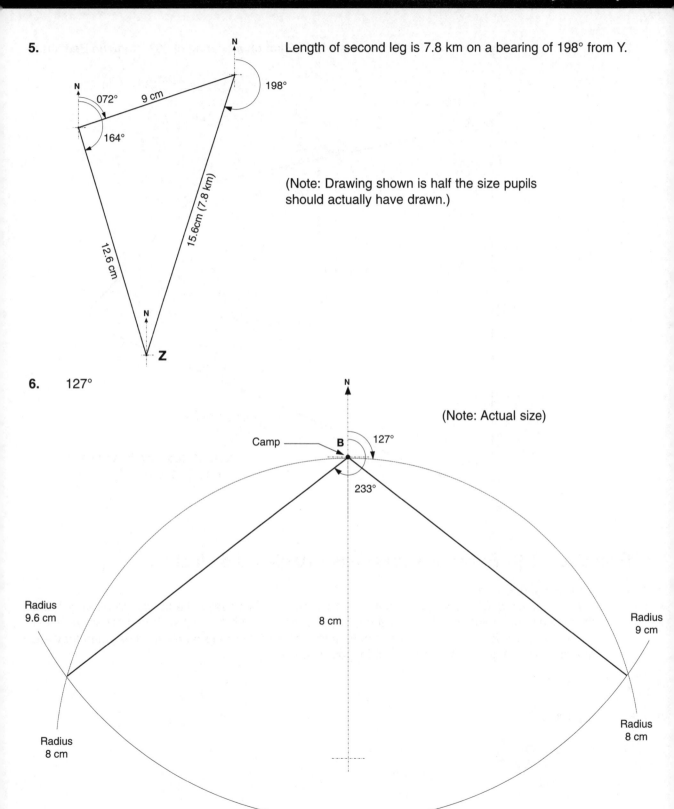

Could have met in one of two places: 233° from B or 127° from B.

7.

The lifeboat travels 12.2 km on a bearing of 067° from the Beeport.

102°

A

8 cm

138°

1 cm to 1 km

5 cm

10 cm

12.2 cm (12.2 km)

(Note: Actual size based on a scale of 1 cm to 1 km)

067°

B

Exercise 12.9: Extension questions – Angles and algebra

1. 3 o'clock and 9 o'clock.

If you work this question out you find that at $16\frac{4}{11}$ minutes past twelve the hands will be at 90°, and thus if the hands rotate continuously then this, and other answers, are also correct. However most clocks have hands that move on the minute, and therefore there are no other times when they are at exactly 90°. A good discussion point for your scholars!

2. (a) $6m$

(b) $120 + \dfrac{m}{2}$

(c) $6m = 120 + \dfrac{m}{2}$

$m = 22$

(d) 4:22

(e) 83.5°

3. (a) $b + 180$ (b) yes   (c) $b - 180$ (d) $b - 180$

4. $90 + \dfrac{x+y}{2}$

5. (a) $\dfrac{180-x}{2}$ (c) $y = \dfrac{180-x}{2}$ (e) $z = 135 - \dfrac{x}{4}$

     (b) y (d) $180 - 2y = \dfrac{180-x}{2}$

6. (a) (i) 50°   (ii) 140°   (iii) 120°

     (b) (i) 40°   (ii) 130°   (iii) 105°

     (c) (i) $\dfrac{360-x}{2}$ (ii) $180 - \dfrac{x}{2}$ (iii) $\dfrac{720-3x}{4}$

Exercise 12.10: Summary exercise

1. (a)

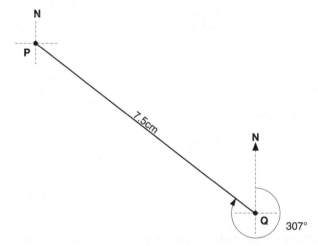

     (b) 307°

2. 037°

3. (a) 170°   (b) 050°

4. (a)-(b)

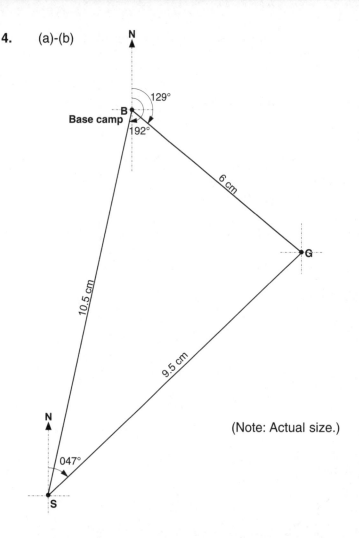

(Note: Actual size.)

(c) 9.5 ÷ 5 → 1.9 km   (pupils may have measured 9.6 cm) Simon has to walk 1.9 km.
(d) Simon has to walk in the direction of 047° (+ or – 1°).

End of chapter 12 activity: Black-eyed Jack's treasure

This activity provides plenty of scope for pupils to use their imagination. Most will enjoy drawing their own plans or maps with suitable hair-raising hazards.

Chapter 13: Area

Exercise 13.1

1.
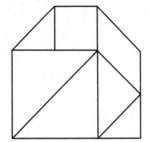

2.
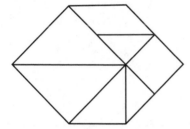

3.
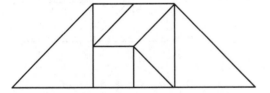

4.
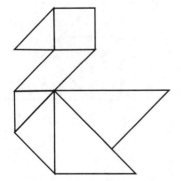

5. Check pupils' own designs.

6. Check pupils' own designs.

Exercise 13.2

1.

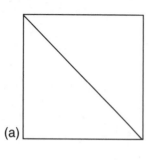 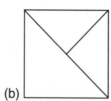 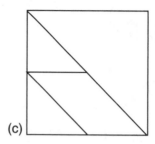

(a) (b) (c)

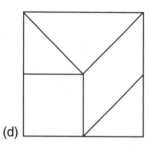

(d) (e) Not possible.

2. (a) 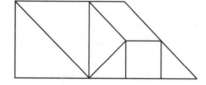 (b)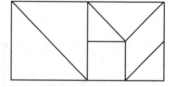

(c) 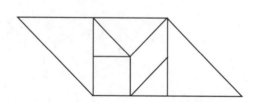 (d)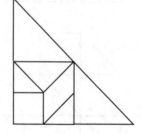

Exercise 13.3

1.	96 cm²		**4.**	450 cm²
2.	240 m²		**5.**	1.44 m²
3.	2.4 m²		**6.**	7200 cm²

Exercise 13.4

1. 24 cm²
2. 80 cm²
3. 0.72 m²
4. 2600 cm²
5. 8.4 m²
6. 6 m²
7. 14 m²
8. 1.56 m²

Exercise 13.5

Warning: These answers depend on the worksheets having been printed at 100% (i.e. not enlarged or reduced to fit paper size). See instructions on the Worksheet CD.

1.-2.	(a)	Base: 6 cm	Height: 3.15 cm	Area: 9 cm²
	(b)	Base: 4.4 cm	Height: 2.8 cm	Area: 6.16 cm²
	(c)	Base: 7 cm	Height: 3.5 cm	Area: 12.25 cm²
	(d)	Base: 3.5 cm	Height: 5.1 cm	Area: 9 cm²
	(e)	Base: 5.4 cm	Height: 3.8 cm	Area: 10.3 cm²
	(f)	Base: 5.5 cm	Height: 3.7 cm	Area: 10.18 cm²
	(g)	Base: 6.6 cm	Height: 4.1 cm	Area: 13.5 cm²
	(h)	Base: 8 cm	Height: 2.6 cm	Area: 10.4 cm²

Exercise 13.6

1. 10
2. 10
3. 10
4. 10
5. 10
6. 10

Exercise 13.7

1. (a) 15 cm² (c) 175 cm²
   (b) 12 cm² (d) 27 cm²

2. 2.5 cm²
3. (a) 16 m² (b) 416 m²
4. (a) 1.73 cm². (b) 10.38 cm².

5.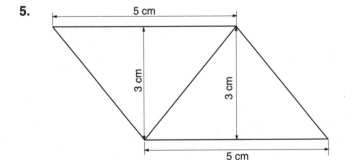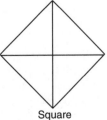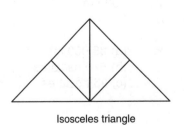

Square   Isosceles triangle

Exercise 13.8

1. 4cm
2. 4cm
3. 6 cm
4. (a) 6cm   (b) 18 cm²   (c) 30 cm²
5. 16 cm

Exercise 13.9

1. 120 cm²
2. 7.2 m²
3. 10.8m²

4. 4.62 m²
5. 8568 cm²
6. 1888 cm²

7. 48.75 cm²
8. (a) 21 m²   (b) 2.5 m   (c) 20 m²   (d) 41 m²

Exercise 13.10

1. (a) 25 m²   (c) 150 cm²
   (b) 500 mm² (5 cm²)   (d) 3600 mm² (0.36 cm²)

2. (a) 37.5 cm²   (b) 48 cm²

Exercise 13.11: Extension questions – Units of area

1. (a) 100   (c) 1 000 000   (e) 0.000 001
   (b) 1 000 000   (d) 0.0001   (f) 0.000 001

2. (a) 160 000 cm²   (b) 0.000 016 cm²

3. (a) 7 500 000 cm²   (b) 75 000 km²

4. (a) 12 000 cm²   (b) 1.2 m²

5. 10 cm
6. 50 metres
7. 2000 m
8. 5 cm

9. (a) 36 000 m²
   (b) 570 hectares
   (c) 96 hectares

10. (a) 500 m
(b) 12.5 and 17.5 hectares.
(c) 7:5
(d)

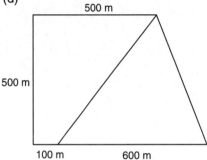

11. The areas are both 0.54 km²

Exercise 13.12: Mixed questions

1. (a) $A = bh$ (b) $A = \dfrac{bh}{2}$ (c) $A = \dfrac{h(a=b)}{2}$

2. (a) 80 cm²   (b) 1.5 m²
3. 12 cm.
4. 588 cm²
5. (a) (i) 72 m²   (ii) 48 m²   (b) 120 m²
6. 2475 mm²

End of chapter 13 activity: The shape game

Practical
This is a useful activity for boosting the pupils' knowledge of shape properties.

Chapter 14: Straight line graphs

Exercise 14.1

1.

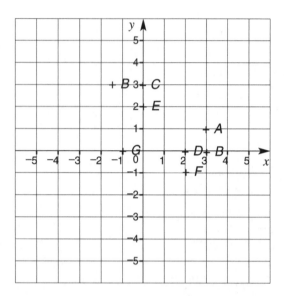

2.   B, D, G
3.   C, E, I

Exercise 14.2

1.   A(−3, 2)   B(−1, 2)   C(1, 2)   D(4, 2)
     y = 2

2.   E(−2, 5)   F(−2, 3)   G(−2, 2)   H(−2, −1)
     x = −2

3.   E(2, 4)   F(2, 2)   G(2, 1)   H(2, −1)
     x = 2

4.   A(−2, −2)   B(0, 2)   C(2, −2)   D(4, −2)
     y = −2

5.   A(−2, 4)   B(0, 4)   C(2, 4)   D(4, 4)
     y = 4

6.   E(4, 3)   F(4, 1)   G(4, −1)   H(4, −3)
     x = 4

7.   E(4, 4)   F(2, 2)   G(1, 1)   H(−1, −1)
     y = x

8.   A(−3, 3)   B(−1, 1)   C(2, −2)   D(3, −3)
     y = −x

Exercise 14.3

1. These two lines intersect at (3,−1)

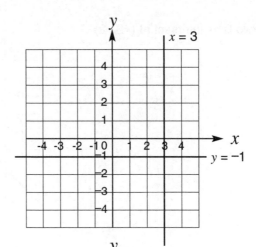

2. These two lines intersect at (−2,0)

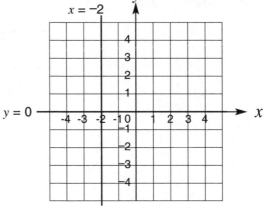

3. These two lines intersect at (4,1)

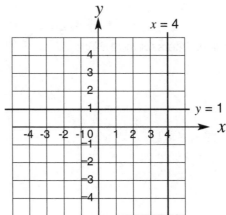

4. These two lines intersect at (−2,−2)

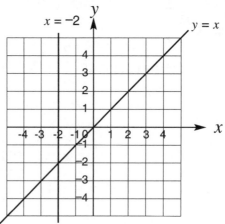

5. These two lines intersect at (0,3)

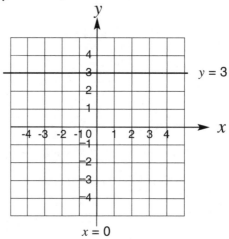

6. These two lines intersect at (2,−2)

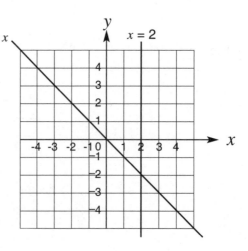

Exercise 14.4

1. 9 sq units

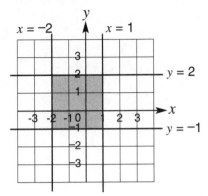

2. Rectangle, 35 sq units

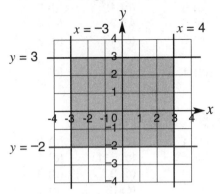

3. Square, 25 sq units

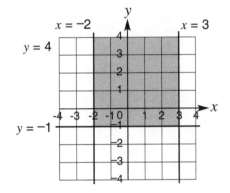

4. 0.5 or $\frac{1}{2}$ sq unit

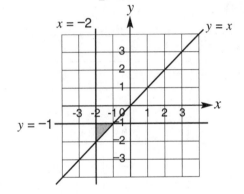

5. $x = 4$

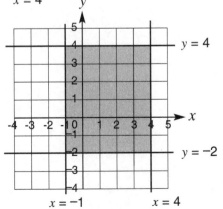

6. $y = 4$

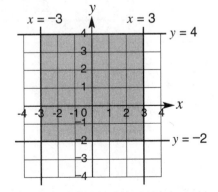

Area of the square is 36 square units.

Exercise 14.5

1. (a) 6 (b) 12 (c) 3 (d) 0
2. (a) 8 (b) 5 (c) 12 (d) 7
3. (a) 3 (b) 5 (c) 7 (d) 4
4. (a) 5 (b) 9 (c) 17 (d) 3

5. (a) 2 (b) 1 (c) 0 (d) $\frac{1}{2}$

Exercise 14.6

1. (a) 1 (b) 4 (c) −2 (d) 0
2. (a) −8 (b) −2 (c) −11 (d) 1
3. (a) −1 (b) 2 (c) 3 (d) 0
4. (a) 3 (b) 5 (c) 2 (d) 1
5. (a) 4 (b) 1 (c) 10 (d) −5

Exercise 14.7

1. (a)

x	−2	−1	0	1	2
y	−4	−3	−2	−1	0

(b)

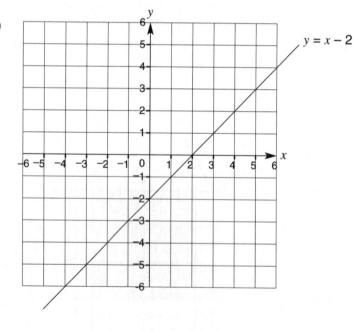

$y = x - 2$

2. (a)

x	−2	−1	0	1	2
y	−3	−1	1	3	5

(b)

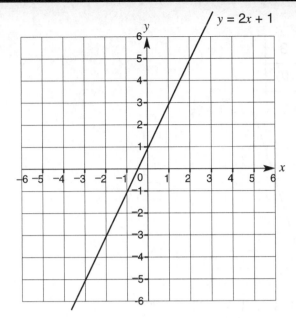

$y = 2x + 1$

(c) (i) 4   (ii) $\frac{1}{2}$

3. (a)

x	−2	−1	0	1	2
y	5	4	3	2	1

(b)

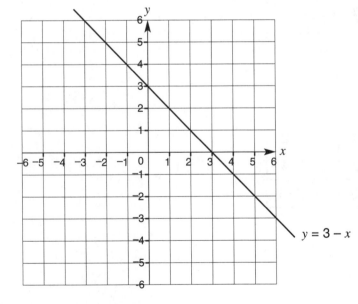

$y = 3 - x$

(c) (i) 3.5   (ii) $\frac{1}{2}$ (0.5)

4. (a)

x	−1	0	1	2	3
y	−2	1	4	7	10

(b)

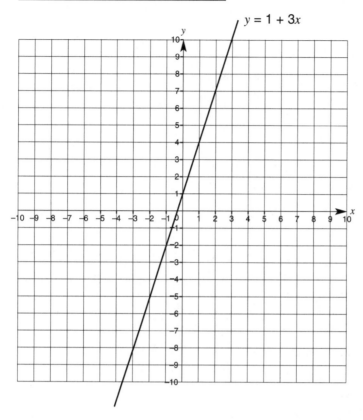

$y = 1 + 3x$

(c) (i) 8.5   (ii) 1.33

5. (a)

x	−2	−1	0	1	2
$2x$	−4	−2	0	2	4
y	−7	−5	−3	−1	−1

(b)

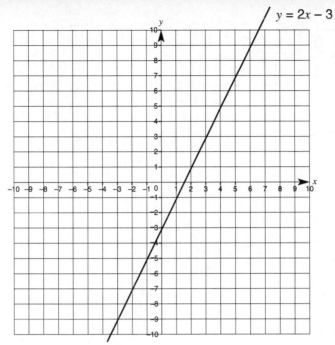

$y = 2x - 3$

(c) (i) 0   (ii) $\frac{1}{2}$ (0.5)

6.   (a)

x	−2	−1	0	1	2
$2x$	−4	−2	0	2	4
y	8	6	4	2	0

(b)

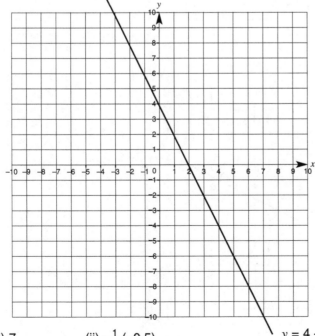

$y = 4 - 2x$

(c) (i) 7   (ii) $-\frac{1}{2}$ (−0.5)

7. (a)

x	−3	−2	−1	0	1	2	3
y	$3\frac{1}{2}$	3	$2\frac{1}{2}$	2	$1\frac{1}{2}$	1	$\frac{1}{2}$

(b)

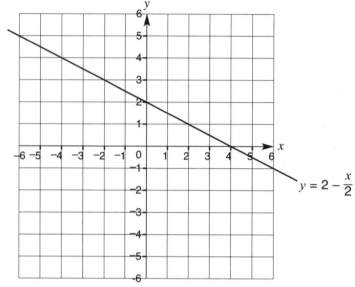

$y = 2 - \dfrac{x}{2}$

(c) (i) 1.25   (ii) 5.55

8. (a)

x	−3	−2	−1	0	1	2	3
y	$-4\frac{1}{2}$	−4	$-3\frac{1}{2}$	−3	$-2\frac{1}{2}$	−2	$-1\frac{1}{2}$

(b)

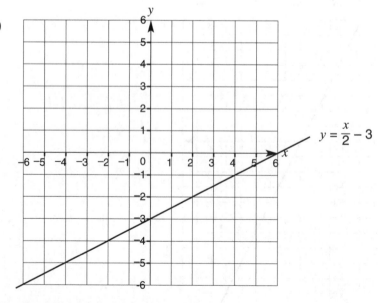

$y = \dfrac{x}{2} - 3$

(c) (i) −2.25   (ii) 3

Exercise 14.8: Extension Exercise

1. (−2,2), (0,3), (2,4), (4,5) $y = \dfrac{x}{2} + 3$

2. (−1,−1), (1,3), (2,5) $y = 2x + 1$

3. (−3,4), (−2,3), (−1,2), (0,1), (1,0), (2,−1), (3,−2) $y = 1 - x$

4. (−2,6), (−1,4), (0,2), (1,0), (2,−2) $y = 2 - 2x$

5. (−2,4), (0,3), (2,2), (4,1) $y = 3 - \dfrac{x}{2}$

6. The number term should be where the line cuts the y-axis

7. The positive x terms slope up to the right and the negative ones slope up to the left.

8. The higher the coefficient of x the steeper the line.

9. (a)-(b)

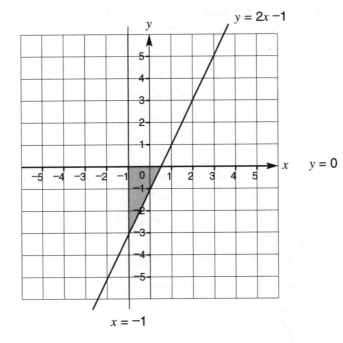

(c) $2\dfrac{1}{4}$ sq units

10. (a)-(b)

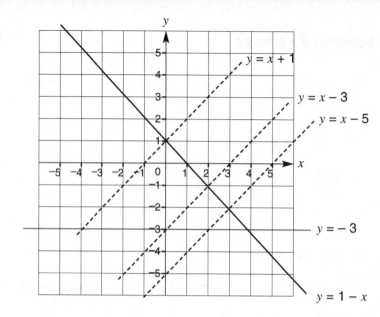

(c)-(e) There is no single correct answer – there are numerous possibilities. Check pupils' answers. Possible answers are shown above with broken lines.

11. (a)-(c)

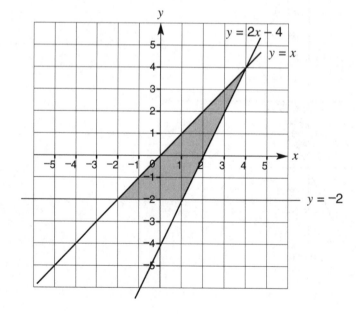

(d) $y = -2$

Exercise 14.9: Summary exercise

1. (a) 9   (b) −5   (c) 7   (d) −1   (e) −3   (f) 6   (g) 7

2.

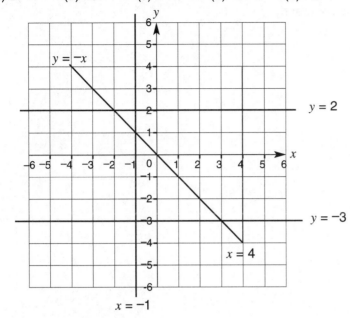

3. (a)

x	−2	−1	0	1	2
$2x$	−4	−2	0	4	2
y	−8	−6	−4	−2	0

(b)

(c) (i) (2,0)   (ii) $y = (0,−4)$

(d) (i) $x = −1$ (ii) $x = 1.75$

End of chapter 14 activity: Real life graphs

This activity provides a good opportunity to explore graphs in magazines and newspapers and for some cross-curricular work with science and geography.

Chapter 15: More About Numbers

Standard Index form is covered in this chapter. Although it is not on the syllabus calculators may still give answers in this form. For many pupils it may not be relevant and does not need to be covered by all.

Exercise 15.1

1.	(a) 105.6	(b) 105.61	(c) 105.615
2.	(a) 2.7	(b) 2.71	(c) 2.714
3.	(a) 0.4	(b) 0.38	(c) 0.375
4.	(a) 6.1	(b) 6.06	(c) 6.057
5.	(a) 14.9	(b) 14.91	(c) 14.905
6.	(a) 25.0	(b) 25.01	(c) 25.008
7.	(a) 0.0	(b) 0.04	(c) 0.044
8.	(a) 0.0	(b) 0.02	(c) 0.021
9.	(a) 4.6	(b) 4.56	(c) 4.556
10.	(a) 1.0	(b) 1.00	(c) 1.000
11.	(a) 10.1	(b) 10.09	(c) 10.091
12.	(a) 200.0	(b) 200.00	(c) 200.000

Exercise 15.2

It is important that the position of 0 is discussed before doing this exercise. Pupils need to understand when it is significant and when it is not.

1.	(a) 500	(b) 0.03	(c)30	(d) 0.003
2.	(a) 400	(b) 0.002	(c) 4	(d) 0.000 7
3.	(a) 50	(b) no hundredths	(c) no thousands	(d) 0.008
4.	(a) 70	(b) 0.000 02	(c) 400	(d) 0.000 000 8

Exercise 15.3

1.	(a) 200	(b) 300 000	(c) 0.05	(d) 0.3
2.	(a) 3100	(b) 950	(c) 0.076	(d) 0.31
3.	(a) 25 100	(b) 3490	(c) 0.005 89	(d) 0.460
4.	(a) 34 600	(b) 120 500	(c) 0.035 47	(d) 0.339 5
5.	(a) 2.00	(b) 25.0	(c) 1.00	(d) 100
6.	(a) 0.0509	(b) 305 000	(c) 0.100	(d) 55.1

Exercise 15.4

1.	(a) (i) 0	(ii) 1	(iii) 3	(iv) 2
	(b) (i) 3	(ii) 2	(iii) 5	(iv) 3
2.	(a) (i) 3	(ii) 2	(iii) 6	(iv) 6
	(b) (i) 3	(ii) 2	(iii) 4	(iv) 3

3.   (a) (i) 0   (ii) 4   (iii) 3   (iv) 5
       (b) (i) 5   (ii) 5   (iii) 5   (iv) 6

4.   (a) (i) 0   (ii) 4   (iii) 3   (iv) 6
       (b) (i) 2   (ii) 3   (iii) 5   (iv) 7

5.   (a) 2.398 for example   (b) 2.0695 for example

Exercise 15.5

1. 10^5
2. 10^2
3. 10^{-2}
4. 10^{-4}
5. 10^8
6. 10^{-9}

7. 10^4
8. 10^{-3}
9. 10^9
10. 10^{-5}
11. 10^{-1}
12. 10^0

Exercise 15.6

1. 2×10^5
2. 2×10^{-6}
3. 3×10^{-1}
4. 5×10^{-3}
5. 6×10^{-9}
6. 4×10^8

7. 9×10^{-6}
8. 2×10^{-5}
9. 2×10^2
10. 8×10^{-13}
11. 5×10^3
12. 3×10^4

Exercise 15.7

1. 700
2. 8 000 000
3. 0.9
4. 500
5. 900 000
6. 30

7. 0.002
8. 70 000 000
9. 0.000 08
10. 0.004
11. 6 000 000
12. 0.02

Exercise 15.8

1. 450
2. 2300
3. 18 200
4. 734 000
5. 0.902

6. 0.0371
7. 0.0041
8. 0.000 672
9. 5450
10. 0.0365

Exercise 15.9

1. 4.2×10^2
2. 1.2×10^4
3. 2.34×10^8
4. 1.02×10^5
5. 3×10^3

6. 5.5×10^1
7. 6×10^{11}
8. $1.990\ 9 \times 10^4$
9. 3.4×10^5
10. 5.06×10^6

11.	3×10^{-3}	**16.**	9.712×10^{-3}
12.	4.51×10^{-3}	**17.**	$1.056\,7 \times 10^{-1}$
13.	5.6×10^{-5}	**18.**	3.05×10^{2}
14.	7.05×10^{-7}	**19.**	6.79×10^{7}
15.	1.2×10^{-1}	**20.**	4.556×10^{-5}

Exercise 15.10

1. 4×10^{6} mm
2. 6×10^{3} grams.
3. 8.64×10^{4}
4. 5×10^{-6}
5. 5×10^{-6}
6. 4.24×10^{-6}
7. 1.5×10^{8} dollars
8. 9×10^{-5}
9. 1.5×10^{8}
10. 1.5×10^{-11}
11. 10 000 000 000 (ten thousand million)
12. 6.694×10^{21} tonnes
13. 8.99×10^{-5}
14. 0.000 000 000 34 m

Exercise 15.11

Answers may vary a little depending on the approximations made.

1. 320 000
2. 120 000
3. 32 000 000
4. 900 000
5. 15 m, 6×1.5 m.
6. £40
7. 50
8. 20 hours
9. 30 hours
10. 200 words per minute

Exercise 15.12: Extension questions

Answers will depend on pupils' initial estimates (and then approximations).

Exercise 15.13: Summary exercise

1.	(a) 19.4	(b) 19.41	(c) 19.409
2.	(a) 7.0	(b) 7.05	(c) 7.050
3.	(a) 300	(c) 300	
	(b) 305	(d) 305.0	

4.   (a) 0.004   (c) 0.004 1
         (b) 0.004 10   (d) 0.004 098
5.   (a) 10^7 (b) 10^{-6} (c) one thousand million
6.   (a) 1700   (c) 0.000 006 3   (e) 810 000
         (b) 6 025 000   (d) 0.000 095 1   (f) 0.005 804
7.   (a) 5.6×10^7 (c) 2.4×10^{-4} (e) 4.05×10^9
         (b) 4×10^{-3} (d) 3.1205×10^7 (f) $5.012\ 3 \times 10^{-4}$
8.   3.5 millimetres
9.   (a) 5×10^6 (b) £500 000
10. Check pupils' own estimates

End of chapter 15 activity: Calculator games

It takes a bit of time getting into this game but then it is a very good way of emphasising what happens when you multiply and divide by 10, 100, 1000 etc.

Chapter 16: Circles

Exercise 16.1
1. 2. 3.   Practical
4.   The pupils should get approximately 3

Exercise 16.2

1.   (a) 24.8 cm (b) 62 m   (c) 31 cm   (d) 12.4 m   (e) 37.2 cm (f) 155 cm

2.   (a) 22 cm   (b) 66 m   (c) 176 mm (d) 88 m   (e) 154 cm   (f) 8.8 m

3.   (a) 10.1 cm (b) 29.5 m   (c) 96.8 mm (d) 1.41 m   (e) 4.40 km   (f) 471 cm

Exercise 16.3
1.   40 100 km
2.   8.80 m
3.   18.8 cm
4.   264 cm
5.   113 cm
6.   25.1 cm

Exercise 16.4
1. 2. 3.   Practical
4.   All the results should be approximately 3.

Exercise 16.5
1.   (a) 616 cm^2 (b) 38.5 m^2 (c) 6.16 cm^2
2.   (a) 77.5 cm^2 (b) 310 m^2 (c) 446 mm^2
3.   (a) 9.62 cm^2 (b) 51.5 m^2 (c) 1060 mm^2
     (d) 707 cm^2 (e) 1590 m^2 (f) 177 cm^2

Exercise 16.6
1.   50.3 cm^2
2.   113 cm^2, 37.7 cm,
3.   38.5 cm^2
4.   (a) 7.07 m^2 (b) 9.42 m
5.   20
6.   6.91 cm^2

Exercise 16.7

1. (a) 726.1 cm²   (b) 5654.9 cm²
    (c) 4.9 m²   (d) 61.3 cm²

Exercise 16.8

1. (a) 115.7 cm   (b) 298.2 cm
    (c) 7.5 m   (d) 241.6 cm

2. (a) 5.09 m²   (b) 9.25 m

Exercise 16.9: Extension questions – The history of π

1. 3
2. 3.160 494
3. 3.141 667
4. 3.141 593
5. (a) 3.0625   (b) 3.1416   (c) 3.162 278
6. 3.140 676
7. 3.136 155
8. Even up to the 10th term the value is still not very accurate. (3.232316)
9. 3.302394 after 7 terms
10. 3.141593

Exercise 16.10: Summary exercise

1. 198cm
2. 154 cm²
3. (a) 31.42 cm   (b) 227 cm²
4. (a) 1.5 cm²   (b) 5041
5. 60.85 cm
6. 145 cm² to 3 s.f.

End of chapter 16 activity: Drawing spirals

Spirals in nature can be explored as part of this topic. It is interesting to be able to relate the mathematical to the geometric. This is good preparation for the work on sequences.

Chapter 17: Transformations

Exercise 17.1

1.

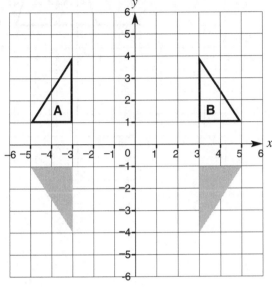

2.

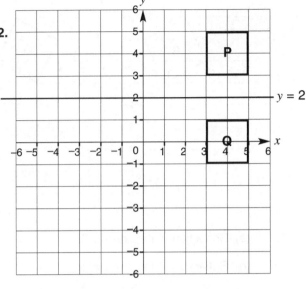

3.

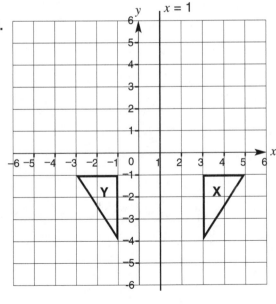

4.

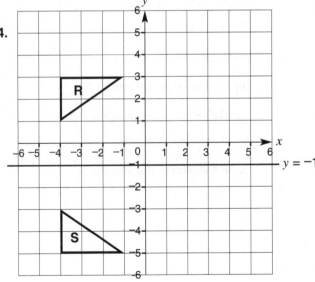

5.

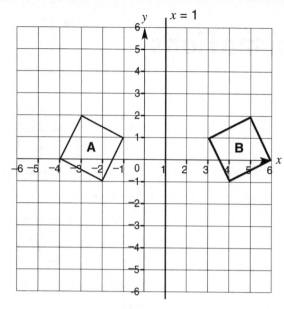

6.

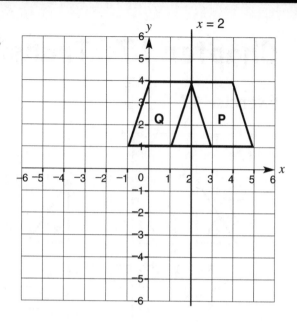

7.　(a) Reflection in the line $x = 0$

　　(b) Reflection in the line $y = 1$

　　(c) Reflection in the line $x = \dfrac{1}{2}$

　　(d) Reflection in the line $y = -\dfrac{1}{2}$

8.　(a) Reflection in the line $x = -1\dfrac{1}{2}$

　　(b) Reflection in the line $x = 0$

　　(c) Reflection in the line $x = 2\dfrac{1}{2}$

　　(d) Reflection in the line $y = 1$

　　(e) Reflection in the line $y = 1\dfrac{1}{2}$

Exercise 17.2

1. (a)-(c)

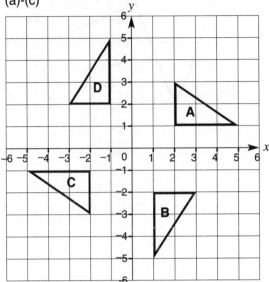

2. (a)-(c)

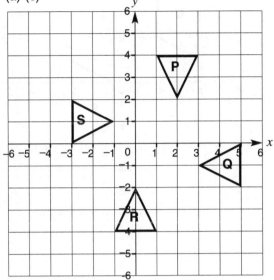

3. (a)-(c)

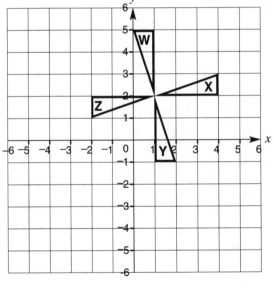

4.

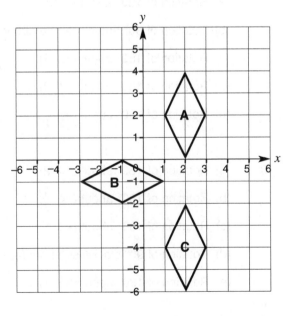

5.

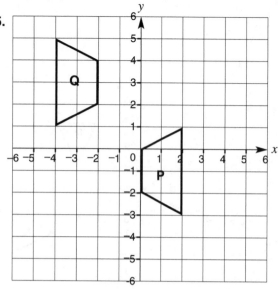

6.

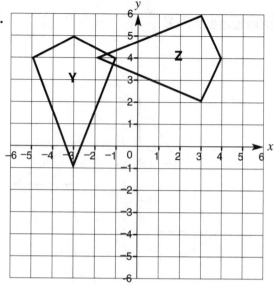

7.   (a) Rotation of 180° about (3, 3)

       (b) Rotation of 90° anti-clockwise about (−2, 1)

       (c) Rotation of 180° about (−2, 2)

       (d) Rotation of 180° about (−1, 2)

       (e) Rotation of 180° about $(2\frac{1}{2}, \frac{1}{2})$

8.   (a) Rotation of 180° about (−4, 2)

       (b) Rotation of 180° about $(-4, \frac{1}{2})$

       (c) Rotation of 180° about (−2, 1)

       (d) Rotation of 90° clockwise about (0, −2)

       (e) Rotation of 180° about $(3\frac{1}{2}, 1)$

9.   A rotation of 180° about the same point.

10.   A reflection in the line $y = 2$

Exercise 17.3

1. (a) By the vector $\begin{pmatrix} 6 \\ -1 \end{pmatrix}$

(b) By the vector $\begin{pmatrix} 5 \\ 5 \end{pmatrix}$

(c) By the vector $\begin{pmatrix} 5 \\ -2 \end{pmatrix}$

(d) By the vector $\begin{pmatrix} 0 \\ -7 \end{pmatrix}$

(e) By the vector $\begin{pmatrix} -6 \\ 8 \end{pmatrix}$

2. (a) By the vector $\begin{pmatrix} 6 \\ -1 \end{pmatrix}$

(b) By the vector $\begin{pmatrix} 3 \\ 0 \end{pmatrix}$

(c) By the vector $\begin{pmatrix} 6 \\ 5 \end{pmatrix}$

(d) By the vector $\begin{pmatrix} 0 \\ -6 \end{pmatrix}$

(e) By the vector $\begin{pmatrix} 7 \\ -1 \end{pmatrix}$

(f) By the vector $\begin{pmatrix} -7 \\ 7 \end{pmatrix}$

3. (a)-(c)

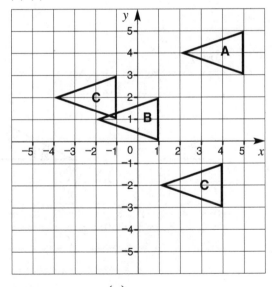

(d) By the vector $\begin{pmatrix} 1 \\ 6 \end{pmatrix}$

4. (a)-(c)

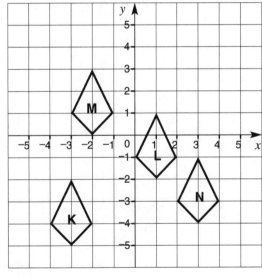

(d) By the vector $\begin{pmatrix} 3 \\ -2 \end{pmatrix}$

Exercise 17.4

1. (a) Reflection in the line $y = 1$

(b) Rotation of 180° about (−1, −2) or 90° anticlockwise (−1, 1)

(c) Translation by the vector $\begin{pmatrix} 1 \\ 4 \end{pmatrix}$

(d) Enlargement by scale factor 2 centre (0, 1)

2.   (a) Reflection in the line $y = 2$; or rotation of 180° about (0, 2)
     (b) Rotation of 90° clockwise about (−4,−2)

   (c) Translation by the vector $\begin{pmatrix} 6 \\ -1 \end{pmatrix}$

   (d) Rotation of 180° about $(-1, -1\frac{1}{2})$

3.   (a) Enlargement by scale factor 2 centre (−5, 3)
     (b) Rotation of 180° about (−1, 3)
     (c) Reflection in the line $y = 1$

   (d) Translation by the vector $\begin{pmatrix} 3 \\ -4 \end{pmatrix}$

   (e) Reflection in the line $x = \dfrac{1}{2}$

   (f) Rotation of 180° about $(\frac{1}{2}, 1)$

4.   (a) Reflection in the line $x = 1$
     (b) Enlargement by scale factor 2 centre (1, 1)
     (c) Rotation of 90° anti-clockwise about (1, 1)

   (d) Translation by the vector $\begin{pmatrix} -1 \\ -6 \end{pmatrix}$

5.   (a)-(c)

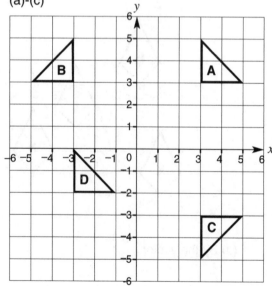

6.   (a)-(c)

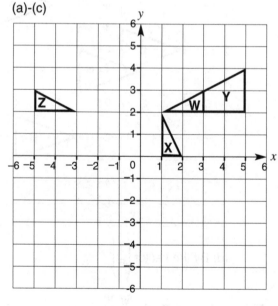

   (d) Rotation of 180° about origin (0, 0)
        or reflection in the line $y = x$

7. (a)-(c)

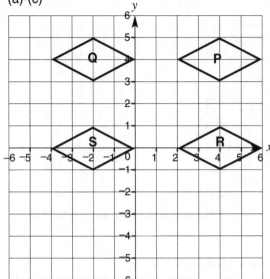

(d) Rotation of 180° about (1, 2)

or translation by the vector $\begin{pmatrix} 5 \\ -4 \end{pmatrix}$

(e) Translation by the vector $\begin{pmatrix} 0 \\ 4 \end{pmatrix}$

or rotation of 180° about (−2, 2)
or reflection in the line $y = 2$

8. (a)-(c)

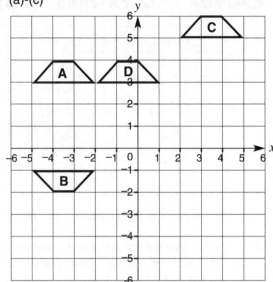

(d) Reflection in the line $x = -2$

(e) Rotation of 180° about (−2, 1)

9. (a), (b), (d) and (e)

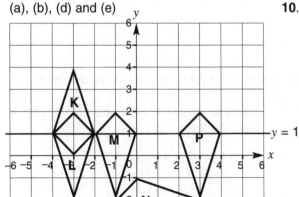

(c) Translation by the vector $\begin{pmatrix} 2 \\ 0 \end{pmatrix}$ or reflection in the line $x = -2$

(f) Rotation of 90° clockwise about
(3, −2) or reflection in the line $y = 1 - x$

10. (a)-(c)

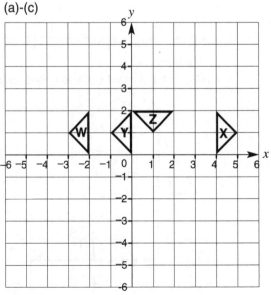

Exercise 17.5: Extension questions

1.

Object	1st Image	2nd Image
(0, −2)	(−2, 0)	(2, 0)
(0, 2)	(2, 0)	(−2, 0)
(−2, −2)	(−2, −2)	(2, 2)
(2, 4)	(4, 2)	(−4, −2)
(2, 2)	(2, 2)	(−2, −2)
(6, 2)	(2, 6)	(−2, −6)

In $y = x$ co-ordinates swap over (are reversed). The $y = -x$ swap over and change their sign.

2.　(a) It could be a rotation but it has no centre.
(b) A reflection in the x axis. The rotation of 90∞ anti-clockwise about (−1,4)
(c) There are several possible answers. e.g. reflection in y axis is followed by a rotation of 90° clockwise about (4,1).
(d) There are several possible answers. e.g. reflection in $y = 2$ followed by a rotation of 90° clockwise about (1,6)

3.　(a) Reflection in $x = -1$
Rotation of 180° about (−1, 4)
Rotation of 90° clockwise about (−1, 1)
Rotation of 90° anti-clockwise about (−1, 7)

Translation by the vector $\begin{pmatrix} 6 \\ 0 \end{pmatrix}$

(b) Reflection in $x = 1$
Rotation of 90° clockwise about (1, −2)

(c) Reflection in $x = -1$
First pair have most because squares have 4 lines of symmetry and rotational symmetry.

4.

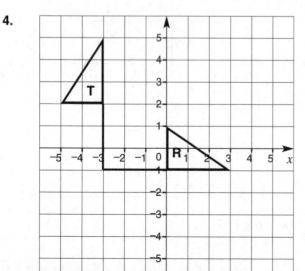

Possible solutions to the second part of this question are:

(i) Reflect R in the line
$y = -1$
Reflect T in the line
$y = x + 2$

or

(ii) Reflect R in the line
$y = x + 2$
Reflect T in the line
$x = -1$

5. (a) Reflection in the line FC.
(b) Rotation of 60° anti-clockwise about E.
(c) Several possible answers, including: reflection in AC to ΔQ, or rotation of 120° anti-clockwise about the centre.
(d) All except ΔT and ΔV
    N by a reflection in BE
    P by a rotation of 180° about the right-angled vertex
    Q by a reflection in AC
    R by a rotation of 60° clockwise about A
    S by a reflection in AD
    T n/a
    U by a rotation of 60° anti-clockwise about C
    V n/a
    W by a rotation of 120° clockwise about the centre

Exercise 17.6: Summary exercise

1. (a) Reflection in $y = 2$ or rotation of 90° anti-clockwise about (−2, 2)
(b) Enlargement by scale factor 2 centre (4, 0)
(c) Rotation of 180° about (3, 3)
(d) Rotation of 180° about (3, 0)

(e) Translation by the vector $\begin{pmatrix} 0 \\ 6 \end{pmatrix}$

(f) Translation by the vector $\begin{pmatrix} -6 \\ -4 \end{pmatrix}$

2. (a)-(c)

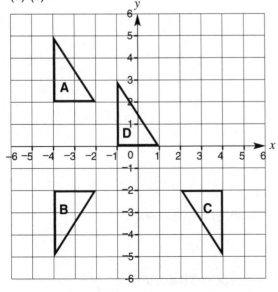

3. (a)-(c)

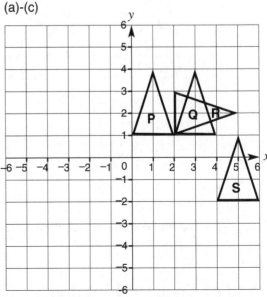

4. (a)-(c)

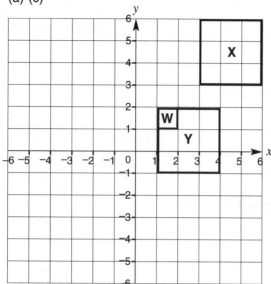

(c) An enlargement by scale factor 3, centre (1, 2)

5. (a)-(c)

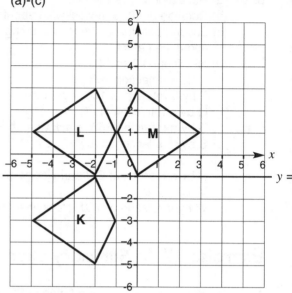

(c) Rotation of 180° about (−1, −1)

6. (a)-(c)

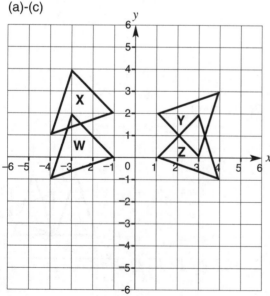

(d) The transformation that maps W to Z is a reflection in $x = 0$ (y axis)

End of Chapter 17 activity: The four colour theorem

See pupils' answers. Check they have not coloured two adjacent regions the same colour.

Chapter 18: Volume

Exercise 18.1

1. (a) 105 cm³   (b) 600 m³   (c) 1.536 m³

2. (a) 125 cm³   (b) 125 000 cm³   (c) 0.125 cm³.

3. (a) 129 600 cm³   (b) 5.376 cm³   (c) 2.16 m³

4. 1200 litres

5. 9 litres

6. They all have a volume of 125 litres

7. (a) 5000   (b) 500   (c) 50

8. 224 millilitres

9. A cube of side 8 cm (512 ml) is larger than half a litre, or a cuboid with sides 5cm, 9 cm and 11 cm (495 ml)

10. (a) $1 \times 1 \times 24$, $1 \times 2 \times 12$, $2 \times 2 \times 6$, $1 \times 3 \times 8$, $1 \times 4 \times 6$, $2 \times 2 \times 6$, $2 \times 3 \times 4$ You can make 6 cuboids.
    (b) $1 \times 1 \times 36$, $1 \times 2 \times 18$, $1 \times 3 \times 12$, $1 \times 4 \times 9$, $1 \times 6 \times 6$
    $2 \times 3 \times 6$, $3 \times 3 \times 4$, $2 \times 2 \times 9$, $1 \times 6 \times 6$ You can make 9 cuboids.
    (c) $1 \times 1 \times 35$, $1 \times 5 \times 7$ You can make 2 cuboids.
    (d) $1 \times 1 \times 37$ You can make 1 cuboid.

Exercise 18.2

1. 5 cm

2. (a) 7 cm   (b) 7.5 cm   (c) 600 cm

3. 5 cm

4. 120 cm

5. (a) 10 cm   (b) 25 cm   (c) 10 cm

6. 20 cm

7. 2.5 cm

Exercise 18.3

1. 225 ml of banana milkshake for 75p (cost 33.3 pence per ml. A smoothie is 34.3 pence per ml)
2. Another shampoo for £1.50 a litre
3. Yes, a box of muesli is better value
4. 80 cm
5. 0.10 g per cubic cm
6. 30
7. (a) 64 (b) 27
8. 0.625 cm (just over 6 mm)

The following exercises on prisms are only an introduction. Volume of a prism is not on the syllabus for papers 1 and 3 of Common Entrance, but the concept helps to reinforce the concept of volume.

Exercise 18.4

1. (a) 15 cm² (b) 15 cm³ (c) 105 cm³ (d) 150 cm³ (e) 78 cm³

2. (a) 80 cm³ (b) 40 cm³ (c) 320 cm³ (d) 1024 cm³

3. (a) 0.9 cm³ (b) 5.4 cm³ (c) 18 cm³

4. (a) 4 000 000 cm³ (b) 80 000 cm³ (c) 80 litres

Exercise 18.5

1. 480 cm³
2. 120 cm³
3. 48 cm³
4. 93 m³
5. 8 cm²
6. 20 cm

Exercise 18.6: Extension questions – Maximum volume

This is an excellent exercise to do using a spreadsheet programme, such as Excel.

1.

x	$8 - 2x$	$10 - 2x$	Volume
1	6	8	48
1.5	5	7	52.5
2	4	6	48
2.5	3	5	37.5
3	2	4	24
3.5	1	3	10.5

2.

x	$20 - 2x$	$20 - 2x$	Volume
1	18	18	324
1.5	17	17	433.5
2	16	16	512
2.5	15	15	562.5
3	14	14	588
3.5	13	13	591.5
4	12	12	576
4.5	11	11	544.5
5	10	10	500
5.5	9	9	445.5
6	8	8	384
6.5	7	7	318.5
7	6	6	252
7.5	5	5	187.5
8	4	4	128
8.5	3	3	76.5

As the results are not symmetrical about the highest value suggest that the pupils draw a graph of their results.

3.

x	$15 - 2x$	$20 - 2x$	Volume
1	13	18	234
1.5	12	17	306
2	11	16	352
2.5	10	15	375
3	9	14	378
3.5	8	13	364
4	7	12	336
4.5	6	11	297
5	5	10	250
5.5	4	9	198
6	3	8	144

4. x against Volume.

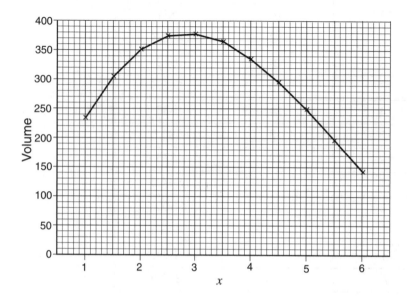

5.

x	$21 - 2x$	$29 - 2x$	Volume
1	19	27	513
1.5	18	26	702
2	17	25	850
2.5	16	24	960
3	15	23	1035
3.5	14	22	1078
4	13	21	1092
4.5	12	20	1080
5	11	19	1045
5.5	10	18	990
6	9	17	918
6.5	8	16	832
7	7	15	735

Maximum volume 1092

6.

x	x^2	$4x^2$	$80 - 4x^2$
1	1	4	76
1.5	2.25	9	71
2	4	16	64
2.5	6.25	25	55
3	9	36	44
3.5	12.25	49	31

Exercise 18.7: Summary exercise

1. 216 cm³
2. 4 cm
3. (a) 360 000 cm³   (b) 360 litres
4. (a) 5 000 000 cm³   (b) 5 m³
5. 4 cm
6. (a) 8100 cm   (b) 8.1 litres
7. 1.6 m
8. 2 litres of DAX at £3.10
9. 480
10. 105 cm³

End of chapter 18 activity: Euler's Theorem

If you have access to polydrons then it makes this investigation much easier.

Name	Faces	Edges	Vertices
tetrahedron	4	6	4
Pyramid	5	8	5
Cube	6	12	8
Octahedron	8	12	6
Dodecahedron	12	30	20
Icosahedron	20	30	12

Therefore **F + V = E + 2**

Chapter 19: More data

The exercises in this chapter deal with grouped data and more awkward numbers. While this is not necessary for the Common Entrance syllabus it is helpful to cover before dealing with any realistic statistical project, such as Geography fieldwork. The section on scatter graphs needs to be covered by everyone.

Exercise 19.1

1. **(a)**

Rainfall in April	Tally	Frequency
0 – 0.9	IIII II	7
1.0 – 1.9	IIII I	6
2.0 – 2.9	IIII IIII	9
3.0 – 3.9	IIII I	6
4.0 – 4.9		0
5.0 – 5.9	I	1
6.0 – 6.9	I	1
Total		30

(b)

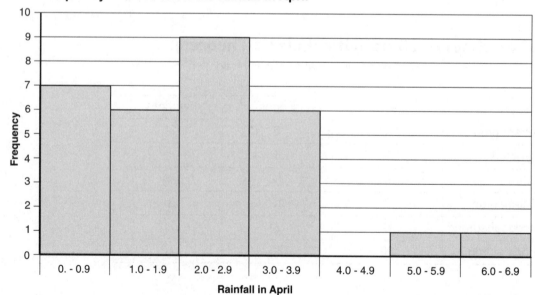

A frequency chart to show the rainfall in April

2.

Rainfall in June	Tally	Frequency
0 – 0.9	◇◇ ◇◇ II	12
1.0 – 1.9	◇◇ III	8
2.0 – 2.9	◇◇ II	7
3.0 – 3.9	III	3
4.0 – 4.9		0
5.0 – 5.9		0
6.0 – 6.9		0
Total		30

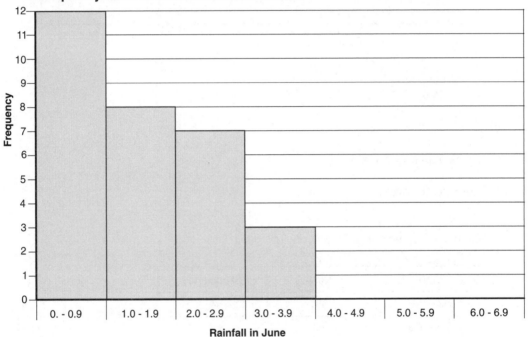

A frequency chart to show the rainfall in June

3. April-Range = 6.7 Mean = 2.17 (to 2 d.p.)
June-Range = 3.2 Mean = 1.37
In June the weather is drier, with less total rain and more dry days. April has more wet days and more rain overall.

4. (a) 40

(b) **A frequency diagram to show the results of a breath holding experiment**

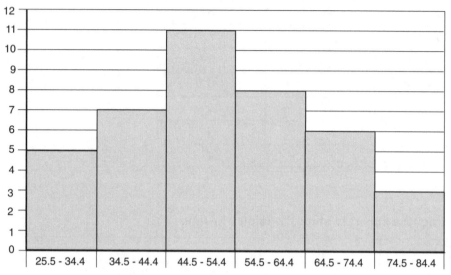

Time in seconds

(c) 44.5 – 54.4

(d) $\frac{11}{40}$

(e) Check pupils' own results

(f) Check pupils' own results

5. (a) Mean = 73%, median = 73.5%

(b)

Mark	Tally	Frequency
50 – 59	IIII	4
60 – 69	IIII III	8
70 – 79	IIII IIII I	11
80 – 89	IIII I	6
90 – 99	III	3
Total		32

(c) 70-79%

(d)

A frequency diagram to show the results of a maths exam

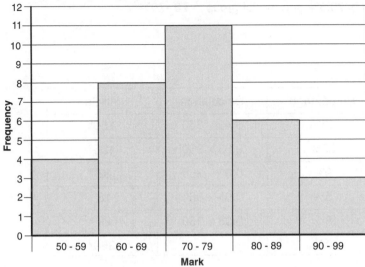

(e)

Mark	Tally	Frequency
50 – 59	ⵜ llll	9
60 – 69	ⵜ ⵜ llll	14
70 – 79	ⵜ ⵜ ⵜ	15
80 – 89	ⵜ ll	7
90 – 99	lll	3
Total		48

A frequency diagram to show the results of a maths exam

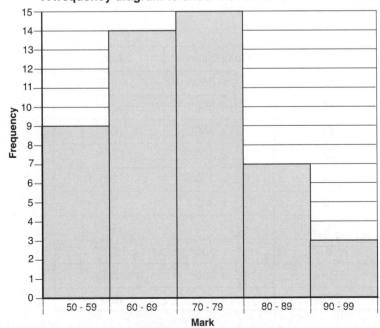

(f) Almost all the new marks are under 75 so this moves the graph more to the lower values.

(g) Mean is 70%, median is 70.5% and modal group is 70 -79%.

Exercise 19.2

1. (a)

Programme	Percentage	Calculation	Angle
Enemies	43%	0.43 × 360	155°
Cuffy	35%	0.35 × 360	126°
The Bob	9%	0.09 × 360	32°
The News	5%	0.05 × 360	18°
Other	8%	0.08 × 360	29°
Total	100%		360°

(b)

A pie chart to show pupils favourite television programmes

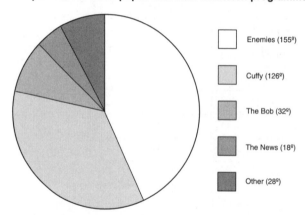

Enemies (155º)

Cuffy (126º)

The Bob (32º)

The News (18º)

Other (28º)

2. (a)

Activity	Number	Calculation	Angle
Television	53	$\frac{53}{220} \times 360°$	87°
Computer	46	$\frac{46}{220} \times 360°$	75°
Sport (F/R)	35	$\frac{35}{220} \times 360°$	57°
Sport (T/B)	22	$\frac{22}{220} \times 360°$	36°
Riding	14	$\frac{14}{220} \times 360°$	23°
Reading	12	$\frac{12}{220} \times 360°$	20°
Art etc	8	$\frac{8}{220} \times 360°$	13°
Music	6	$\frac{6}{220} \times 360°$	10°
Other	24	$\frac{24}{220} \times 360°$	39°
Total	220		360°

(b)

A pie chart to show how pupils spend their free time

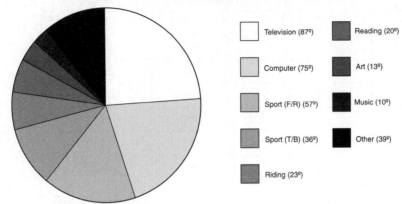

Television (87º)   Reading (20º)

Computer (75º)   Art (13º)

Sport (F/R) (57º)   Music (10º)

Sport (T/B) (36º)   Other (39º)

Riding (23º)

(c) 10%
(d) 45%
(e) $\frac{7}{110}$

3. (a)

Activity	Number	Calculation	Angle
Curried eggs	53	$\frac{53}{190} \times 360°$	100°
Mushy peas	45	$\frac{45}{190} \times 360°$	86°
Spring Greens	36	$\frac{36}{190} \times 360°$	68°
Fish cakes	21	$\frac{21}{190} \times 360°$	40°
Cheese pie	15	$\frac{15}{190} \times 360°$	28°
Spinach pie	12	$\frac{12}{190} \times 360°$	23°
Other	8	$\frac{8}{190} \times 360°$	15°
Total	190		360°

(b)

A pie chart to show the least liked school lunches

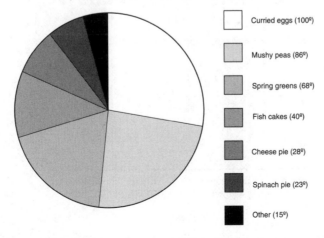

Curried eggs (100º)

Mushy peas (86º)

Spring greens (68º)

Fish cakes (40º)

Cheese pie (28º)

Spinach pie (23º)

Other (15º)

(c) 28%   (d) 43%   (e) $\frac{5}{90} \rightarrow \frac{3}{38}$

4. (a)

Activity	Amount	Calculation	Angle
Cake stand	53	$\frac{53}{267} \times 360$	71.5°
Washing cars	25	$\frac{25}{267} \times 360$	34°
Silence	44	$\frac{44}{267} \times 360$	59.5°
B and buy	61	$\frac{61}{267} \times 360$	82°
Walk	72	$\frac{72}{267} \times 360$	97°
Face painting	12	$\frac{12}{267} \times 360$	16°
Total	267		360°

(b)

A pie chart to show the results of how money was raised for charity

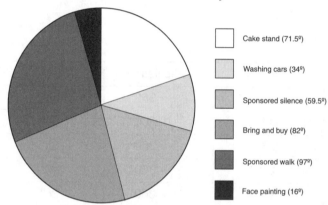

Cake stand (71.5º)

Washing cars (34º)

Sponsored silence (59.5º)

Bring and buy (82º)

Sponsored walk (97º)

Face painting (16º)

(c)

A bar chart to show the results of how money was raised for charity

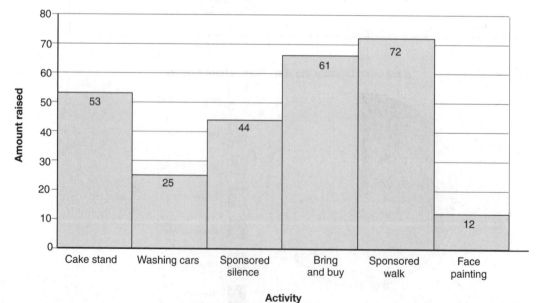

(d) Check pupils' own answers. A pie chart shows comparative values better, and a bar chart absolute values better.

Exercise 19.3

1. This graph shows a positive correlation.

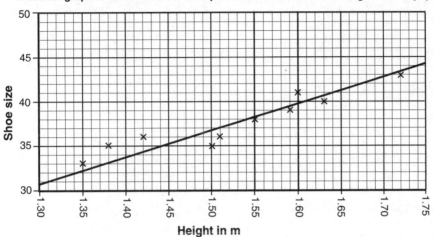

A scatter graph to show the relationship between shoe sizes and heights of ten pupils

2. Check pupils' own comments.

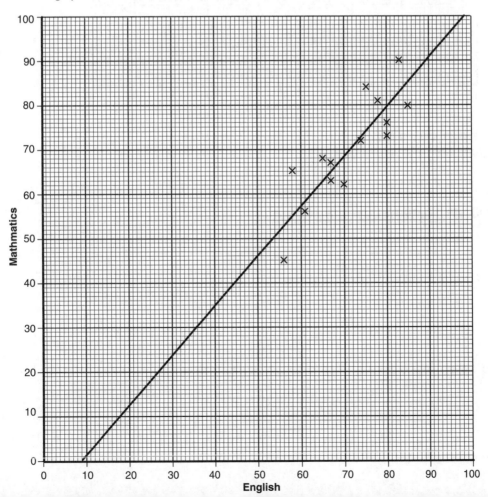

A scatter graph to show the relationship between the marks scored in Maths and English exams

3. Check pupils have drawn lines of best fit on graphs 1 and 2 (see previous page).

4. (a)

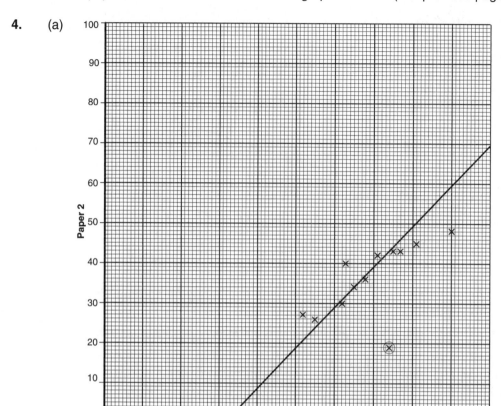

(b) See the point circled in graph above.
(c) See graph above for line of best fit.
(d) 47%

Exercise 19.4: Extension questions

1. $20x$

2. $125x$

3. (a) $\dfrac{1980}{x}$ (b) $\dfrac{165}{x}$

4. $x = 13$

5. (a) 0. (No eleven year olds give 12 children with a total age of 120 → average 10 exactly.)
(b) 19, 7   (c) 5, 17

6. (a) 1   (b) none

7. 21

8. (a) $\frac{x}{12}$ (b) $\frac{x}{12} = 19$ 228

9. (a) $1.75x$ (b) $\frac{3x}{4}$ (c) $\frac{1}{9}$

(d)

Days off	0	1	2	3	4	5
people	$\frac{x}{4}$	$\frac{x}{3}$	$\frac{x}{6}$	0	$\frac{x}{6}$	$\frac{x}{12}$

(e) $\frac{x}{4} - 24 = \frac{x}{12}$ 144

Exercise 19.5: Summary exercise

1. (a)

Rainfall	Tally	Frequency
0 – 0.9	ℍℍ ℍℍ IIII	14
1.0 – 1.9	III	3
2.0 – 2.9	IIII	4
3.0 – 3.9	ℍℍ	5
4.0 – 4.9		0
5.0 – 5.9	III	3
6.0 – 6.9	I	1
Total		30

(b)

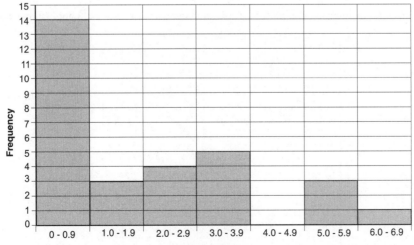

A frequency diagram to show the daily rainfall in September

(c) Range is 6.3 cm, mean is 1.90 cm to 2 d.p.

2. (a)

Activity	Amount	Calculation	Angle
More than 10	17	$\frac{17}{175} \times 360°$	35°
8 or 9	25	$\frac{25}{175} \times 360°$	51.5°
6 or 7	20	$\frac{20}{175} \times 360°$	41°
4 or 5	58	$\frac{58}{175} \times 360°$	119°
2 or 3	43	$\frac{43}{175} \times 360°$	88.5°
Less than 2	12	$\frac{12}{175} \times 360°$	25°
Total	175		360°

(b)

A pie chart to show the results of how many books children read this term

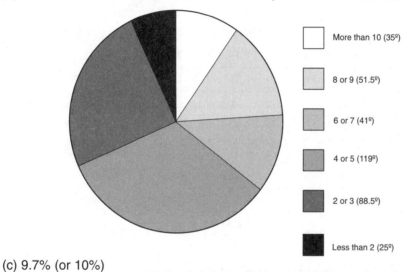

☐ More than 10 (35º)

◻ 8 or 9 (51.5º)

◻ 6 or 7 (41º)

◻ 4 or 5 (119º)

◼ 2 or 3 (88.5º)

■ Less than 2 (25º)

(c) 9.7% (or 10%)

3. (a)

A scatter graph to show the comparison of weights against the masses of people in my class

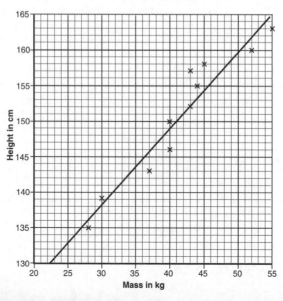

(b) See graph above for line of best fit.
(c) About 43 kg

End of chapter 19 activity: A Fibonnacci number trick

This starts with a way to multiply by 11, then the 'trick' is fun for those that like such things, but possibly not for everyone. The algebra is also interesting for the more able.

Chapter 20: Algebra 3 – More equations

Exercise 20.1

1. 4
2. 6
3. 7
4. 4
5. 5

6. 3
7. 3
8. 2
9. 1
10. 2

Exercise 20.2

1. 5
2. 10
3. 5
4. 4
5. 7

6. 7
7. 2
8. 5
9. −9
10. 3

Exercise 20.3

1. −5
2. 4
3. −11
4. 6
5. −10

6. −3
7. 3
8. −2
9. −1
10. −4

11. $\frac{2}{3}$
12. $3\frac{1}{2}$
13. $-1\frac{1}{2}$
14. $\frac{4}{5}$
15. $-2\frac{1}{5}$

16. $2\frac{1}{2}$
17. $\frac{5}{6}$
18. −1
19. $-3\frac{1}{2}$
20. $-2\frac{1}{2}$

Exercise 20.4

1. −4
2. $1\frac{2}{3}$
3. −8
4. $-1\frac{1}{3}$
5. 1

6. $1\frac{1}{3}$
7. $\frac{5}{11}$
8. $1\frac{2}{5}$
9. $\frac{1}{3}$
10. $\frac{1}{4}$

11. $1\frac{1}{11}$

12. $1\frac{4}{5}$

13. $\frac{4}{9}$

14. $-\frac{1}{4}$

15. -1

16. $\frac{1}{16}$

17. $4\frac{1}{4}$

18. $-\frac{3}{13}$

19. -1

20. $\frac{13}{22}$

Exercise 20.5

1. 2

2. 3

3. $1\frac{2}{3}$

4. 20

5. 3

6. 2

7. $-\frac{1}{3}$

8. $6\frac{1}{2}$

9. 2

10. 26

11. $2\frac{1}{3}$

12. 4

13. -14

14. $2\frac{1}{2}$

15. $\frac{1}{5}$

16. -1

17. -1

18. $-2\frac{1}{2}$

19. $-1\frac{1}{8}$

20. $-\frac{1}{5}$

Exercise 20.6

1. (a) $4x$ (b) $2x + 30$ (c) $2x + 30 = 4x$, $x = 15$ (d) 15p, 60p

2. (a) $4x + 72$ (b) $5x + 36$ (c) $4x + 72 = 5x + 36$, $x = 36$ (d) £1.80

3. $2x + 30 + x = 180$, $x = 50$

4. (a) $6x - 42$
   (b) $6x - 42 = 180$, 37°, 56°, 87°

5. (a) $x - 5$
   (b) $x + 10$
   (c) $2x - 5 = x + 10$, $x = 15$
   (d) 50 cm

6.   (a) $x + 10$, $x - 2$
   (b) $3x + 8$
   (c) $4x$
   (d) $3x + 8 = 4x$, £8, £18, £6

7.   (a) $3x$
   (b) $x + 15$
   (c) $x + 15 = 4x$, 5, 15, 20

8.   (a) x
   (b) $x - 4$
   (c) $2x - 8$ or $2(x - 4)$
   (d) $3x - 8 = 28$, 12 years and 8 years

9. $10x - 8 = 52$, 19 cm and 7 cm

10. $2x + 9 = 3x - 1$, 841 cm²

11.   735

12.   18p, 24p

Exercise 20.7: Extension questions

1.   (a) 10 # 6

   (b) (i) 3   (ii) 19   (iii) 4   (iv) 1   (v) 5   (vi) 4

2.   (a) (ii) $-5 \ddagger -2$ (iii) $2 \times 3 \ddagger 3^2$

   (b) (i) 42   (ii) -8 (iii) -1 (iv) 3   (v) $-\frac{1}{6}$

3.   (a) (i) $4 \triangle 6$ (iii) $\frac{1}{2} \triangle -1$

   (b) (i) $1\frac{1}{2}$ (ii) 10   (iii) 1   (iv) $1\frac{1}{4}$ (v) -1 (vi) -2

4.   (a) (i) $1 \lozenge 19$ and (iii) $3 \lozenge 3$

   (b) No. Only if y is negative.

   (c) (i) 27   (ii) 26   (iii) 23

   (d) $3 \lozenge 12$, $6 \lozenge 24$

Exercise 20.8: Summary exercise

1. (a) −3   (b) 11   (c) 1   (d) $-\frac{1}{4}$ (e) $1\frac{2}{3}$ (f) 2

2. (a) (i) $2x$ (ii) $x + 10$
    (b) $3x + 7 = x + 10$, Charlie has 1.5 Euros
    (c) 23 Euros

3. (a) $5x + 8$ (b) $4x + 12$ (c) $5x + 8 = 4x + 12$, $x = 4$ pence

4. (a) $2x$

    (b) $10x + 150 = 11x + 55$ Normal price would be £1.90
        $95 = x$ (special offer)

    (c) £11

End of chapter 20 activity: A music genius test

A variation on an old theme, just for fun.

Age Aint **0** But A Number	(Aaliyah)
1 Man Went To Mow	(Trad.)
The Animals Went In **2** By **2**	(Trad.)
I Saw **3** Ships Come Sailing In	(Trad. Carol)
The **4** Seasons	(Vivaldi)
Beethoven's **5**th	(Beethoven)
Five, **6**, Seven, Eight	(Steps)
7 Days	(Craig David)
I'm Henry The **8**th I Am	(Murray/Weston; also Herman's Hermits)
Love Poetica Number **9**	(The Clovers; also Nylon; also film of that title)
10 Green Bottles	(Trad.)
9 O'Clock, **10** O'Clock, **11** O'Clock, Rock	(Bill Haley)
On The **12**th Day Of Christmas	(Trad.)
14 Years	(Guns 'n Roses)
15 Men On A Dead Man's Chest	(Young E. Allison)
I Am **16** Going On **17**	(Rodgers and Hammerstein)
Never Been **21** Before	(Toy Dolls)
24 Hours From Tulsa	(Gene Pitney)
When I'm **64**	(The Beatles)
50 Ways To Leave Your Lover	(Paul Simon)
76 Trombones Led The Big Parade	(M Wilson)
99 Red Ballons	(Nena)
1812 Overture	(Tchaikovsky)

Chapter 21 : Sequences

Exercise 21.1

1. (a) (i)   30, 35, 40,
  (ii) 31, 36, 41,
  (b) (i) $100 \times 5 = 500$
  (ii) $100 \times 5 + 1 = 501$

2. (a) (i)   24, 28, 32,
  (ii) 23, 27, 31,
  (b) (i) $100 \times 4 = 400$
  (ii) $100 \times 4 - 1 = 399$

3. (a) (i)   36, 42, 48,
  (ii) 39, 45, 51,
  (b) (i) $100 \times 6 = 600$
  (ii) $100 \times 6 + 3 = 603$

4. (a) (i)   17, 20, 23,
  (ii) 40, 47, 54,
  (ii) 29, 34, 39,
  (b) (i) $100 \times 3 - 1 = 299$
  (ii) $100 \times 7 - 2 = 698$
  (iii) $100 \times 5 - 1 = 499$

5. (a) (i)   36, 49, 64,
  (ii) 21, 28, 36,
  (ii) 21, 34, 55,
  (b) (i) $10 \times 10 = 100$
  (ii) $1 + 2 + 3 + 4 + 5 + 6 + 7 + 8 + 9 + 10 = 55$
  (iii) 55 is the tenth term

Exercise 21.2

1. (a)

 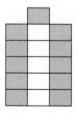

(b)

White rectangles	1	2	3	4	5	100
Green rectangles		5	7	9	11	201

(c) $2 \times 100 + 1$

2. (a)

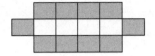

(b)

White rectangles	1	2	3	4	5	10	20
Green rectangles	4	6	8	10	12	22	42

(c) $2 \times 20 + 2$

3. (a)

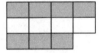

(b)

White squares	1	2	3	4	5	10	20	100
Green rectangles	1	3	5	7	9	19	39	199

(c) $2 \times 100 - 1$
(d) Odd numbers

4. (a)

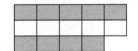

(b)

Pattern number	1	2	3	4	5	10	20	100
lines	4	7	10	13	16	31	61	301

(c) $3 \times 100 + 1$

5. (a)

Pattern 4   Pattern 5

(b)

Pattern number	1	2	3	4	5	10	20	100
lines	6	11	16	21	26	51	101	501

(c) $5 \times 100 + 1$

6. (a)

Pattern 4   Pattern 5

(b)

Pattern number	Green rectangles	White rectangles	Total rectangles
1	1	0	1
2	4	0	4
3	8	1	9
4	12	4	16
5	16	9	25
6	20	16	36
10	36	64	100
100	396	9604	10000

(c) Total is 100 x 100
White is 98×98
Green is the difference

7. (a)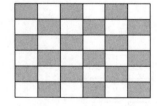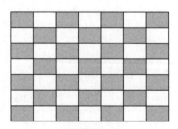

Pattern 4   Pattern 5

(b)

Pattern number	Green rectangles	White rectangles	Total rectangles
1	1	0	1
2	5	4	9
3	13	12	25
4	25	24	49
5	41	40	81
6	61	60	121
10	181	180	361
100	19801	19800	39601

(c) Total is $(2n-1)^2$. Green rectangles are $\dfrac{(2n-1)^2+1}{2}$; White rectangles are $\dfrac{(2n-1)^2-1}{2}$

$100n$ pattern number is therefore

Total is $(200-1)^2$; Green rectangles $\dfrac{(200-1)^2+1}{2}$

and white is the difference $\dfrac{(200-1)^2-1}{2}$

8. Check pupils' own patterns, tables and numbers in their 100th pattern.

Exercise 21.3

1.	(a) 5	(b) 6	(c) 7	(d) 8
2.	(a) 0	(b) 1	(c) 2	(d) 3
3.	(a) 5	(b) 8	(c) 23	(d) 32
4.	(a) 5	(b) 9	(c) 13	(d) 19
5.	(a) 6	(b) 7	(c) 11	(d) 14
6.	(a) 6	(b) 26	(c) 101	(d) 501

Exercise 21.4

1. 14, 17, 20 $T_n = 3n - 1$

2. 26, 31, 36 $S_n = 5n + 1$

3. 18, 22, 26 $V_n = 4n - 2$

4. 33, 40, 47 $U_n = 7n - 2$

5. 27, 33, 39 $S_n = 6n - 3$

6.   Q1. $2n + 1$

Q2. $2n + 2$

Q3. $2n - 1$

Q4. $3n + 1$

Q5. $5n + 1$

Exercise 21.5

1.   25, 36, 49 $S_n = n^2$

2.   26, 37, 50 $T_n = n^2 + 1$

3.   24, 35, 48 $U_n = n^2 - 1$

4.   28, 39, 52 $V_n = n^2 + 3$

5.   Q6. Total is n^2 White is $(n - 2)^2$ Green is the difference or $4n - 4$

Note that this does not work for $n = 1$; it only works for $n > 1$ because $4 \times 1 - 4 \rightarrow 0$, so for Pattern 1 there should be no green rectangles. However there is one white rectangle.

White rectangle $(n - 2)^2$
$$\rightarrow (1 - 2^2)$$
$$\rightarrow (-1)^2$$
$$\rightarrow 1$$

Q7. Total is $(2n - 1)^2$ Green is $\dfrac{(2n-1)^2 + 1}{2}$ White is the difference $\dfrac{(2n-1)^2 - 1}{2}$

Exercise 21.6: Extension questions – A pair of old friends

1.   (a) Question 1(a) was incorrectly given in the first print-run of Maths Book 2 as 2, 5, 7, 12, 19... The next three terms would be 31, 50, 81.

This question will be changed in the reprint of Book 2 to read 0, 2, 5, 9, 14...

The next three terms for this sequence is 20, 27, 35.

For the sequence 0, 2, 5, 9, 14 the rule for the nth term is $\dfrac{1}{2}n(n + 1) - 1$

The sequence 2, 5, 7, 12, 19... is a Fibonnaci style sequence and so there is no formula for the nth term

(b) 21, 28, 36 $\dfrac{1}{2}n(n - 1)$

(c) 42, 56, 72 $n(n + 1)$

2. (a)

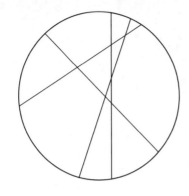

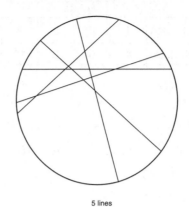

4 lines   5 lines

(b)

No. of lines	1	2	3	4	5	6
No. of regions	2	4	7	11	16	22

(c) $R_n = \frac{1}{2}n(n+1) + 1$

3. (a) 31, 50, 81

(b) 29, 47, 76

(c) 16, 26, 42

4. (a) 2, **3**, 5, 8, 12, **17**, 23, **30**,

(b) 1, 5, **6**, 11, **17**, 28, **45**,

(c) **1**, 7, 17, **31**, 49, 71, **97**,

(d) 50, 32, 18, **8**, 4, **2**, 4, **10**, The difference goes down by 4 each time, but as you are subtracting − −2 it becomes a plus: 50 (−18), 32 (−14), 18 (−10), 8 (−6), 4 (−2), 2 (− −2), 4 (− −6), 10.

Exercise 21.7: Summary exercise

1. (a) (i) 48, 56, 64,   (ii) 45, 53, 61,
(b) (i) 8 ×100 = 800   (ii) 8 ×100 − 3 = 797

2. (a) (i) 59, 69, 79,   (ii) 32, 37, 42,
(b) (i) 10 ×100 − 1 = 999   (ii) 5 ×100 + 2 = 502

3. (a)

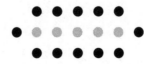

(b)	No. of green dots	1	2	3	4	5	6
	No. of black dots	4	6	8	10	12	14

(c) 22
(d) 49

4. (a) 17 (b) 11 (c) 2 (d) −16

5. 17, 21, 25 $T_n = 4n - 3$

6. 27, 38, 51 $T_n = n^2 + 2$

End of chapter 21 activity: Dot patterns

Number	1st	2nd	3rd	4th	5th	nth
Triangular	1	3	6	10	15	$\frac{1}{2}n(n+1)$
Square	1	4	9	16	25	n^2
Pentagonal	1	5	12	22	35	$\frac{1}{2}n(3n-1)$
Hexagonal	1	6	15	28	45	$n(2n-1)$ or $\frac{1}{2}n(4n-2)$
Heptagonal	1	7	18	34	55	$\frac{1}{2}n(5n-3)$
Octagonal	1	8	21	40	65	$n(3n-1)$ or $\frac{1}{2}n(6n-4)$

There are two possible formulas that could be given for the nth term of the pattern with N sides:

1. $\frac{1}{2}n\left[(N-2)n - (N-4)\right]$

2. $n + \dfrac{(N-2)\,n\,(n-1)}{2}$

Notes

Notes